Frederick the Great
&
the Seven Years' War

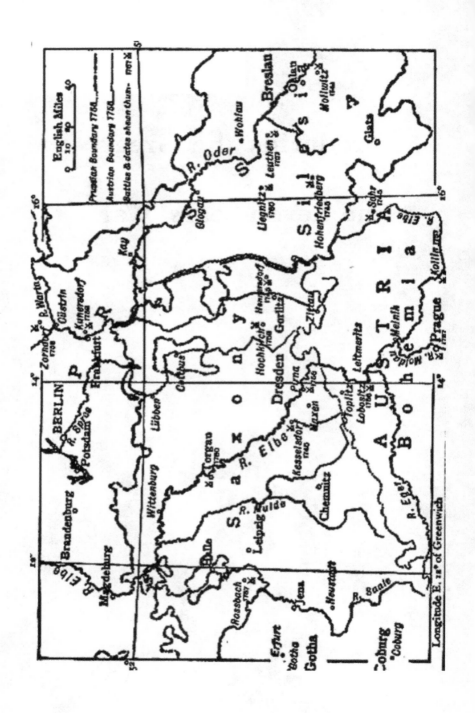

Frederick the Great
&
the Seven Years' War

F. W. Longman

LEONAUR

Frederick the Great & the Seven Years' War
by F. W. Longman

First published under the title
Frederick the Great and the Seven Years' War

Leonaur is an imprint of Oakpast Ltd

ISBN: 978-0-85706-581-0 (hardcover)
ISBN: 978-0-85706-582-7 (softcover)

http://www.leonaur.com

Publisher's Notes

Contents

GERMANY

at the commencement of
THE THIRTY YEARS WAR
1618

English Miles

United Provinces

East Friesland

St of Bremen

Bremen

Luneburg

Oldenburg

Bp of

Bp of

Münster

Bp of

Bp of

Wolfenbüttel

Bp of

Bp of Cologne

Cassel

Hildesheim

Spanish Netherlands

Brussels

Hesse Cassel

Fulda

Siegen

Jülich

Coblenz

Hesse Darmstadt

Lorraine

Ansbach

Furth

Nuren

Neuburg

Helbronn

Wirtemburg

Ulm

Franche Comté

St Gallen

GO

SWISS CONFEDERATION

Graubündten

Wallis

Valtelline

Savoy

Piedmont   Milan   VENICE

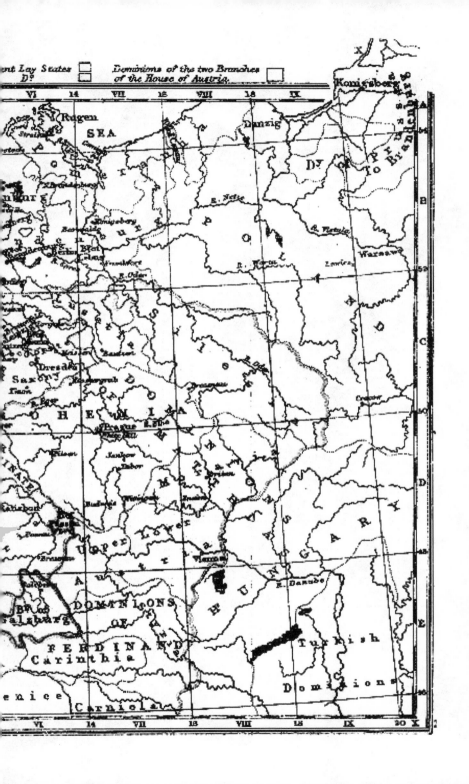

Preface

This book may perhaps be read by some who will desire a fuller knowledge of Frederick the Great, and of the time in which he lived, than can be derived from its pages: for the sake of these I propose to mention a few of the best books on the subject. Anything like an exhaustive list of the authorities I have laid under contribution would be out of place, for, as may well be supposed, in the case of events which happened in a period so near to us as the middle of the eighteenth century, the literature of the subject is very extensive. All I offer, therefore, is a selected list containing the books which appear most likely to be of use.

The first to be mentioned is, of course, Carlyle's *History of Frederick the Great*, a noble work which is appreciated most by those who know it best. Much, however, has been written since the publication of its last volume, especially in Germany, where several books have appeared founded in part on materials that were not accessible to its author.

Foremost among these are Arneth's *Geschichte Maria Theresia's*, a very important work based on documents in the Vienna archives, from which until recently historical enquirers were jealously excluded, and Schafer's *Geschichte des Siebenjährigen Kriegs*, the most accurate and comprehensive history of the war in existence. Some of Ranke's works deal with parts of the subject. For the war itself the professor has only a series of short studies, but its origin is elaborately investigated in his *Ursprung des Sieben-jahrigen Kriegs*. An excellent account of the early part of Frederick's reign and of the history of Prussia, up to the king's accession, will be found in his *Zwölf Bücher Preussicher Geschichte*, while the later policy of Frederick is discussed in *Die Deutschen Mächte und der Fürstenbund*.

To the works of these great modern writers may be added Preuss's well-known biography of Frederick the Great, and the king's own historical writings, of which a separate edition has recently been published in France.

For Ferdinand of Brunswick, and that part of the war in which England was directly concerned, the great authority is Westphalen's *Geschichte der Feldzüge des Herzogs Ferdinand*, but though this work is invaluable to students, it is altogether unsuited to the general reader, who will find Manvillon's biography more adapted to his requirements.

Of contemporary French history most readers will find as much as they want in Voltaire's *Siècle de Louis XV.*, and in either Sismondi or Martin. Several recent publications, such as the Duc de Broglie's *Le Secret du Roi*, and the *Mémoires et Lettres du Cardinal de Bernis*, possess considerable interest, though the amount of new information which they contribute is somewhat less than has been supposed.

For the English history of the period, and for the war regarded from an English point of view, the standard modern work is Lord Mahon's *History of England from the Peace of Utrecht to the Peace of Versailles*, but here it is easier as well as more desirable for the student to bring himself into contact with some of the original authorities. The following may be consulted with advantage: Horace Walpole's *Letters and Memoirs, The Chatham Correspondence, The Annual Register,* and *The Gentleman's Magazine* for the years in question. The Memoirs of Sir Andrew Mitchell, the English ambassador at the Prussian Court, derive great value from the fact that Mitchell accompanied the king throughout the campaigns of the Seven Years' War.

Among later English works, Coxe's *House of Austria*, and Thackeray's *Life of Pitt*, are useful though dull. Several of Macaulay's Essays relate to the period, but that on Frederick is rather to be admired for its brilliancy than commended as trustworthy. Mr. Lecky's *History of England in the Eighteenth Century* will be read with deep interest by such as already possess some knowledge of the period. For America Bancroft's *History of the United States* is the standard work. Readers who desire a more detailed account of the affairs in India will find in Orme the storehouse whence subsequent historians have drawn their materials. The French side of the story is admirably represented in Colonel Malleson's interesting *History of the French in India*.

Chapter 1

Introductory

The importance of the Seven Years' War as an epoch in the history of Europe lies chiefly in its bearing on the question of German unity. The war resulted in placing the young Prussian kingdom on a footing of equality with the old monarchy of the Hapsburgs, and so raising up within Germany a rival and counterpoise to Austria, a rallying point round which all opposition to her might gather. It thus laid the foundations of the unification of Germany, which could never have been effected as long as the Austrian supremacy remained unbroken. For though Austria, before the time of Frederick the Great, was indisputably the greatest of German powers, she was after all more foreign than German. Her external interests in Hungary, Italy, and elsewhere were too extensive for her to care much for the welfare or union of Germany; in fact, the tendency and avowed aim of her policy was to keep it weak and divided. On the other hand, Prussia was thoroughly German; if a large portion of her territory was originally Sclavonic, it had been thoroughly Germanized before the time of Frederick. Her victories first awakened within the German people a yearning for national existence, while her successful resistance to the foreign enemies that Austria arrayed against her marked her out as its fitting leader. The Seven Years' War may therefore be looked upon as the first act of the drama that was played out at Sadowa and Sedan.

It must not be supposed that Frederick had any visions of a united Germany such as now exists, or that he ever consciously aimed at anything of the kind. The chief if not the sole object of his policy, like that of every Hohenzollern before and after him, was the aggrandizement of his own kingdom, and for Germany outside Prussia he cared very little. If on various occasions he appeared as the champion of the smaller German states, that was simply because he desired to limit the influence of Austria in Germany, and to check her encroachments. But it so happened from the nature of the case that the carrying out of his policy necessarily conduced to the future welfare, or at any rate to the independence, of Germany. The aggrandizement of Prussia, whether in territory or influence, could in the main only be effected at the expense of Austria, and what Prussia gained at Austria's expense Germany gained too. Therefore, though Frederick's aims were selfish, he was none the less working for Germany as well as for Prussia, and it would have been a calamity for Germany, and for Europe too, if he had been compelled to succumb to the coalition which the not unreasonable jealousy of Austria directed against him.

True it is that German unity has not been accomplished in a way or with results altogether satisfactory to Germans themselves or to the rest of Europe. For the present, at any rate, Prussia has rather swallowed up Germany than been absorbed in her. But, on the one hand, it must be considered that perhaps in no other way could the fragments have been welded together at all; and, on the other, it may be hoped with some confidence that the present condition of the new Empire is merely a phase due to personal causes which are not likely to be permanent.

In the history of the world the Seven Years' War has a yet wider significance. The war which England waged with France in alliance with Frederick left her the absolute mistress of the seas, gave her the French colonies of North America, and founded her empire in India. It decided the question whether North America and India were to be English or French; and here there is little doubt that the decision was given in the way most accordant with the interests of humanity. Furthermore, the acquisition of Canada by England freed her own colonists from the dread of a powerful and hostile neighbour, and consequently removed their need for dependence on the English Crown. Thus the way was paved for the formation, a few years later, of the United States of America. And this, again, had a considerable influence on the French Revolution.

Chapter 2

Brandenburg and Prussia

§1. Foundation of the Margraviate of Brandenburg.

Prussia is, (at time of first publication), with the exception of Italy, the youngest of the great European powers. Unlike the other states of western Europe, which rose out of the ruins of the old Roman Empire, she grew up amid the decay of the Romano-German Empire. Her development may be traced step by step from the very beginning, and some slight knowledge of it is necessary for a right understanding of her position at the time of the accession of Frederick the Great. The present chapter contains a short account of the Margraviate of Brandenburg and of the Duchy of East Prussia, the union of which in the seventeenth century gave birth to the modern Prussian kingdom.

The early history of Brandenburg is the history of a German colony planted in the midst of a foreign race, of an outpost guarding the north-eastern frontier of the Empire. The year 928 is given as the date of its foundation. In that year the Emperor, or rather, to speak correctly, the German king, Henry the Fowler, marching in winter across the frozen bogs, took Brannibor, a stronghold of the Wends, a tribe of Sclavonian origin inhabiting the lands between the Elbe and the Baltic. The Wends were a barbarous heathen race, and very troublesome neighbours to the more civilized dwellers in the Empire; so Henry appointed a *margrave* (*Markgraf* or Warden of the Marches) to hold them in check and keep order along his frontier. The first headquarters of the *margrave* was Salzwedel, a place on the German side of the Elbe, about sixty miles to the north-west of Brannibor, or Brandenburg as it was afterwards called.

It was not till two centuries later, when the Wends had been brought into tolerable subjection, that the *margraves* took up their residence at Brandenburg. The first of them who did so was Albert, Count of Ascanien and Ballenstädt, surnamed the Bear from the device on his shield,

From Albert's time onwards,(1130-70), the *Margrave* of Brandenburg ranks among the leading princes of Germany, and is recognised as an elector, that is to say, as one of the princes to whom the right of choosing the Emperor belonged.

Under Albert and his descendants Brandenburg grew and prospered till the beginning of the fourteenth century, when the direct line of the house failed, and then followed ninety years of anarchy, under two weak dynasties of electors. At last, after many vicissitudes, the Emperor Sigismund gave it to Frederick of Hohenzollern, *Burggrave* of Nuremberg, in pledge for various sums of money he had advanced. Four years later (April 30, 1415) Sigismund formally conferred the mark and electoral dignity upon Frederick; and with this event the real history of Brandenburg may be said to commence.

The new elector came of a family already distinguished in German history. Its founder was a cadet of the Swabian family of Hohenzollern, named Conrad, who was made *burggraviate* of Nuremberg by the Emperor Frederick Barbarossa, somewhere about the year 1170. Conrad's descendants held the *burggraviate* for two centuries and a half, and gradually acquired large territories in the neighbourhood by purchase or inheritance. Baireuth, Anspach, and Culmbach, afterwards known collectively as Culmbach, thus came into their possession. The activity and energy of the *burggraves*, combined with the importance of their office, the central position of their territories, and the powerful matrimonial alliances which they had made, enabled them to take a prominent part in all affairs of the Empire. Thus, though not electors themselves, they had great influence in the choice of emperors. Rudolph, Count of Hapsburg, the first of that family to attain the Imperial dignity, owed his election to the exertions of one of the *burggraves*.

On his arrival in Brandenburg Frederick found the country in a very disorganized condition, owing to the weakness of its rulers ever since the extinction of the line of Albert the Bear. The nobles, secure in their strong castles, defied the central authority with impunity, in an age when the powers of defence were much stronger than those of attack. The towns, however, were disposed to support him cordially. They had suffered from the turbulence and licentiousness of the nobility, and longed for the establishment of a strong and settled government. By means of artillery, then first coming into use in war, Frederick was able to batter down some of the principal castles, and amongst them the great stronghold of Friesack with walls said to be fourteen feet thick. In the course of a few years, by a judicious mixture of conciliation and severity, he reduced his unruly *vassals* to obedience, and had little further trouble with them for the rest of his reign, (1415-1440).

§2. THE HOHENZOLLERNS IN THE FIFTEENTH AND SIXTEENTH CENTURIES.

Between the death of Frederick I. and the accession of the Great Elector there was an interval of exactly two hundred years, during which nine Hohenzollern electors ruled in Brandenburg, (1440-1460). None of them can be described as really great men, but there was only one of conspicuous feebleness. They seem to have been for the most part hard-headed, energetic, unimaginative men, devoting themselves to the internal administration of their mark, enlarging its borders from time to time and never letting go what they had once fairly grasped. With one or two exceptions they mixed very little in national affairs, and even in the stirring times of the Reformation they played an insignificant part, In common with the majority of North German princes they embraced Protestantism, not indeed with enthusiasm, but after some hesitation, following instead of leading their people. The present greatness of the Hohenzollerns is unquestionably due, in no slight degree, to their having been gradually recognised as the champions of the Protestant religion in Germany; it is therefore worthy of remark that for more than a century after the commencement of the Reformation the electoral branch of the family rendered it no real service.

During this period more interest attaches to the history of the younger branch settled in Culmbach, which produced many men of note in their day, among whom was Albert the Grandmaster (*Hochmeister*) of the Teutonic order, who contributed largely to the rise and progress of his family.

The Teutonic Order, founded at the time of the third Crusade, first rose into distinction early in the thirteenth century, under the Grandmastership of Hermann von der Salza, who undertook the conversion of the heathen Prussians, a Lithuanian tribe inhabiting the plains about the mouth of the Vistula. After the Prussians had been converted or exterminated, the knights took possession of the whole country

15

known at present as East and West Prussia. They also acquired vast property in Germany; but to them, as to the Templars, wealth brought degeneracy. The consequence was that they were worsted after a long struggle with their neighbour, the King of Poland, and forced to cede West Prussia, and to do homage to the Polish Crown for East Prussia, which they were permitted to retain.

The homage was naturally regarded as a grievous indignity, and when Albert was elected to the Grandmastership he had to take an oath to refuse it. This, however, was easier said than done. From the knights who had exacted the oath, or at least from the great body of them scattered through Germany, he received little or no assistance, and he was at last compelled to come to terms with the King of Poland. The king was his mother's brother, and perhaps on that account not indisposed to an amicable settlement of the difficulty. At the Peace of Cracow it was a hereditary agreed that the order was degenerate and unworthy of further existence, and consequently that the Prussian portion of it should be considered as dissolved; further, that Albert should be hereditary Duke of East Prussia, and do homage for it to Poland in that capacity, (1525). This arrangement was facilitated by the fact that Albert had recently, from conviction or interest, become a Protestant. It was of course regarded in Germany as a very nefarious proceeding, and Albert was put to the ban of the Empire; but he was too far off to be easily got at, so he remained in secure possession of his duchy. Some forty years afterwards (1568) the electoral branch of the family obtained the right of succession in the event of male issue failing to Albert, and to the other Culmbachers.

Early in the seventeenth century the whole Culmbach line died out, and the electors of Brandenburg became possessed of East Prussia. At the same time they came into, what was perhaps more important, a well-founded claim to the rich duchies of Cleves and Juliers, Albert's only son having married Maria Eleonora, the eldest daughter of Duke William of Cleves, on whom her father had settled all his lands if the male line of his house should fail. In 1609 the male line did fail, and the whole inheritance ought to have gone to Maria Eleonora and her children. Maria Eleonora herself was dead, but she had left daughters, of whom one was married to the Elector of Brandenburg. The Hohenzollerns claimed the duchies, but their claim was disputed by the Count Palatine of Neuburg, who had married the second daughter of Duke William. There were other competitors, and the affair was not settled till long afterwards, when a compromise was effected by which

16

the inheritance was divided between the two principal claimants, the Duchy of Cleves with the counties of Mark and Ravensburg going to Brandenburg, Juliers and Berg to Neuburg, with a stipulation that if the male line failed in either family the other should have the whole, (1624). This intricate question is of more consequence than perhaps it appears; it is bound up with much of the early history of the Prussian kingdom.

§3. THE GREAT ELECTOR, 1640–88.

In the Thirty Years' War Brandenburg played a thoroughly contemptible part. The shifty and vacillating elector, George William, was unable to attach himself definitely to either side, and saw his lands ravaged by both. Himself a Calvinist, ruling over a Lutheran population, he was the tool of his Catholic Prime Minister, Schwarzenberg. Even when the King of Sweden, the noble Gustavus Adolphus, landed in Germany, and made the cause of German Protestantism his own, he hesitated long before he could make up his mind to a complete breach with Austria. As soon as Gustavus was dead, he abandoned the Swedes, though they had the hearty sympathy of his subjects, and patched up a peace with the Emperor.

Luckily for Brandenburg George William died before the war was quite done, and the reins of government passed into stronger hands. His son and successor, Frederick William, known as the Great Elector, is, with the exception of his great-grandson, Frederick the Great, by far the most remarkable prince of the line of Hohenzollern. Though only twenty years old at the time of his accession, he had long looked with disfavour on his father's aimless policy, and at once set himself to undo its fatal results. By degrees he deprived Schwarzenberg of the almost absolute power he enjoyed, and, after freeing his fortresses from Imperial garrisons, came to terms with the Swedes, and induced them to evacuate the places they still held in Brandenburg.

The gradual formation of a standing army secured for him a consideration which had never been shown to his father, and enabled him at the Peace of Westphalia, (1648), to obtain more favourable terms than could otherwise have been hoped for. It is true that he failed to get the whole of Pomerania, though he had an undoubted right to it in virtue of an old agreement with the dukes of that country, the last of whom died during the war. The justice of his claim was admitted, but the Swedes had got possession of Pomerania, and it was impossible to dislodge them. A compromise had to be made. It was settled that the Swedes should keep Lower Pomerania with Stettin and some other towns that did not properly belong to it. The rest was given to the elector, and to console him for his disappointment the sees of Magdeburg, Halberstadt, and Minden were secularized in his favour, that is to say they were made part of the electoral dominions. He was no loser by the bargain.

The Great Elector is deservedly regarded as the founder of the Prussian monarchy. During his long reign of forty-eight years he re-organized and consolidated his dominions, strengthening the central authority in the various provinces over which he ruled. His chief po-litical success was the extortion from Poland of a complete and formal renunciation of her sovereign rights over his duchy of East Prussia, which was accomplished by taking part first on one side, then on the other, in a war between Poland and Sweden.

In domestic affairs one of his most beneficial measures was the establishment of an excise on articles of consumption in place of the old direct tax on houses and lands, which pressed very heavily on the towns, depopulated as they were by long continued war. Besides being less burdensome to his subjects, the excise was also more profitable to the elector than the old system of taxation, and gave him the means of maintaining a considerable standing army. The maintenance of a standing army in the time of peace was undoubtedly a startling inno-vation, but it was rightly judged by the elector to be indispensable not merely for the security of his own struggling dominions, but also for the protection of the Empire itself against its powerful and ambitious neighbours. His subjects objected to it strongly at first, but they were not insensible to the renown acquired in several successful campaigns, and the elector's victories tended to cement his territories into an united whole, and to inspire them with the feeling that they were all parts of one nation. At the same time he conferred on them benefits more tangible than military glory by draining bogs, cutting canals, bringing waste-lands into cultivation, and other economic measures.

One of the last acts of the elector's life was calculated to teach German Protestants to look upon Brandenburg as their leader and protector. In 1685 Louis XIV. revoked the Edict of Nantes, by which a certain measure of toleration had been secured to the French Prot-estants. Frederick William replied to this arbitrary act by the Edict of Potsdam, which offered a home in Brandenburg to any of the Protes-tants who could effect their escape. This bold measure threatened to disturb the friendly relations which had hitherto subsisted between

Brandenburg and France, and rendered a close alliance with Austria necessary for the former, and thus perhaps explains—what otherwise seems unaccountable—the elector's renunciation for a trifling equivalent of his really considerable Silesian claims.

The Silesian claims were twofold. In the first place there was a claim on the duchies of Liegnitz, Brieg, and Wohlau, which according to an old agreement ought to have fallen to Brandenburg in 1675. In 1537 Joachim II., Elector of Brandenburg, had made with the Duke of Liegnitz an Erbverbrüderung, or compact of inheritance, by which if the duke's line should die out his duchies of Liegnitz, Brieg, and Wohlau were to go to Brandenburg, and in like manner, if the electoral Hohenzollern line should become extinct, certain fiefs of Brandenburg were to go to Liegnitz. Similar arrangements were frequently made by the German princes; but the then Emperor, Ferdinand I., who was also King of Bohemia, protested against this one on the ground that the dukes of Liegnitz had voluntarily constituted themselves vassals of the Bohemian Crown about two centuries before.

That they had done so was perfectly true, but their right to dispose of their territories as they pleased had always been acknowledged, and it seems that Ferdinand had no right whatever to interfere with it. He was, however, strong enough to compel the duke to give up the Erbverbrüderung as far as he himself was concerned, though the elector firmly refused to resign his own claims. Nevertheless when the dukes of Liegnitz became extinct, the Emperor Leopold successfully opposed the succession of the Hohenzollerns. Unwilling to let a strong Protestant power gain a footing in the heart of his hereditary dominions, he took possession of the duchies when they became vacant, and refused to give them up.

In the second place there was a weaker claim on the duchy of Jägerndorf. Early in the sixteenth century Jägerndorf had been granted by the King of Hungary and Bohemia to George of Anspach, one of the Hohenzollerns of Culmbach. On the extinction of the Culmbach line Jägerndorf fell home to the elector of Brandenburg, and was given as an appanage to a junior member of the family named John George. John George took an active part on the anti-imperial side in the Thirty Years' War, and (1623) Jägerndorf was confiscated by the Emperor not altogether in accordance with law and precedent.

Frederick William found, after repeated solicitations, that it was impossible to obtain any of these territories from the Emperor, and at last agreed to resign his claims on them, (1686), and to accept instead a small patch of territory known as the circle of Schwiebus, situated to the north of Silesia on the borders of his own electorate. Schwiebus was accordingly handed over, but the Austrian Court had no intention of permanently giving up even this miserable little bit of territory. It had previously made a secret agreement with the electoral Prince and had induced him to promise that, if his father should accept Schwiebus, he would restore it when he succeeded him as elector.

The prince appears to have been in ignorance of the real strength of the Silesian claims, and to have been led to believe that they were put forward by the French Party in his father's council merely with the view of defeating the Austrian alliance. What induced him to consent to the secret agreement was that, besides being himself really anxious for the alliance, he was anxious to purchase the Emperor's assistance in his domestic affairs. He seems to have feared that his stepmother, who had great influence over the elector, would prevail on her husband to make a will unfavourable to his interests, and providing large appanages for his half-brothers. He might then be glad to have the Emperor's help in setting the will aside. Soon after his accession to the electorate he discovered the deceit that had been practised upon him, and though, for the sake of his promise he restored Schwiebus, he at the same time resumed his claims upon the Silesian duchies.

The position to which Brandenburg had been raised by the Great Elector enabled his son Frederick to demand the Emperor's permission to assume the title of king. (November 16, 1700). The Emperor gave his consent reluctantly. It is said that his ministers were bribed freely, but there is no certain proof of that. What weighed with the Emperor was the advantage of securing Frederick's assistance in the Spanish Succession war, then on the point of commencing; and the price which Frederick demanded for his services was the royal title. The coronation was performed at Konigsberg, the capital city of the duchy of Prussia, which gave its name to the new king. The reason why he took his title from Prussia was that it formed no part of the empire. In Prussia therefore he was an independent sovereign, while in respect of the lands he held in Germany he was a *vassal* of the Emperor.

Frederick's assumption of the royal title is rather a landmark than an epoch in history, but it is a great deal more than a mere landmark. The royal dignity was a source of moral, if not of material strength to the Hohenzollerns. It raised them into the same class as the sovereigns of England and France, and brought them into more or less of a rivalry with the emperors themselves. As Frederick the Great very truly remarked, Frederick I. by erecting Prussia into a kingdom sowed a seed of ambition in his posterity which was certain to bear fruit sooner or later. Prince Eugene was well aware of this when he said that the ministers who advised the Emperor to give his consent to it deserved to be hanged.

CHAPTER 3

The Reign of Frederick William, 1713–40

§1. FREDERICK WILLIAM AND THE ARMY.

The "seed of ambition" bore no fruit in the time of the first king. Frederick I., a man of somewhat feeble character, was satisfied with giving a lustre to his crown by the splendour of his ceremonials. His son and successor was of a totally different stamp. A coarse, uncultivated boor, with a passionate temper, and a touch of insanity, Frederick William had nevertheless considerable merits as a sovereign.

He saw clearly that the dignity of his newly-created kingdom, composed as it was of detached provinces, extending from the borders of France on the west to those of Russia on the east, could only be maintained by an army out of all proportion to its population, and he determined to have it. Frugal and simple in his own life, he could not endure that the wealth of the nation should be squandered on empty show, and he promptly curtailed the expenditure of the Court, which had been very lavish in his father's time, and introduced economy into every branch of the public expenditure.

The resources thus obtained provided the means for adding regiment after regiment to the army, until from the 38,000 which it had numbered at the accession of Frederick William it rose by degrees to nearly 84,000. To give it a national character and to insure its being kept at the required strength, the whole country was divided into circles, and each regiment was assigned to a particular district, from which two-thirds of its members were recruited—by forcible enlistment if necessary.

The recruits for the remaining third were raised by so-called voluntary enlistment in the empire and in foreign countries, or, to speak more correctly, they were in too many cases kidnapped by devices which made the Prussian recruiting sergeant a byword in Europe. Army organization was the one business of Frederick William's life. He took a delight in even the minutest details of the service, and though his mania for tall recruits and the prices he paid for them must provoke a smile, he still deserves great credit for the perseverance with which he went on perfecting the machine until in drill and discipline his army stood far in advance of any in Europe. The efficiency was greatly promoted by the introduction of iron ramrods, an invention of Prince Leopold of Anhalt-Dessau, which enabled the muskets to be loaded more rapidly than was possible with the old wooden ones, and so gave the Prussian soldiers an advantage similar to that which they derived from the needle gun in 1866.

But it was not in Frederick William's time that this superiority was manifested. The eccentric king was too fond of his well-drilled battalions to risk them in battle, and with the exception of a single campaign in Pomerania, he waged no war on his own account, though he had on one occasion to send a contingent to the army of the Empire.

The Pomeranian campaign, (1715), in which he was involved against his will, forms part of the long war between Charles XII. of Sweden and Peter the Great of Russia. Its result for Prussia was the important acquisition of Stettin and some other parts of Swedish Pomerania.

§2. FREDERICK WILLIAM AND THE BALANCE OF POWER.

The reign of Frederick William is an important period in the history of Prussia. It forms the transition from the old condition of entire dependence on the Empire to the complete independence achieved for her by her next sovereign. The change was brought about purely by the force of circumstances, and not at all by any deliberate intention on the part of Frederick William. Though very sensitive about his rights as an independent sovereign, he was devotedly loyal to the Empire, and never forgot that he was a prince of it. It was with great reluctance that he ever placed himself in opposition to the Emperor, badly as the latter often treated him.

The war of the Spanish Succession had just been brought to a close when Frederick William ascended the Prussian throne. The Peace of Utrecht, (April 1715), recognized the claims of Philip of Anjou, the

French claimant of the Spanish crown, but at the same time divested the monarchy of several provinces for the benefit of the Austrian claimant, the Archduke Charles, who, upon the death of his brother Joseph, had become Emperor with the title of Charles VI. Charles thereby received Naples, Milan, the ports of Tuscany, and the Spanish Netherlands, the latter being designed to form a barrier for the protection of Holland against France. England retained Gibraltar and Minorca, which she had conquered during the war. Prussia was recognized as a kingdom by France, and had her borders slightly enlarged by the acquisition of Spanish Guelders.

The peace aimed at preserving a balance of power by preventing either France or Austria from becoming too powerful; but it really left the preponderance with France. France was a compact and homogeneous nation, grown rich and powerful under a strong and settled government. Austria was not a nation at all, but a collection of nationalities, whose sole bond of union lay in the circumstance that they all owed allegiance to the same man. The Empire was dead in all but name.

The strength it seemed still to possess was derived from the power of the House of Austria, from which for nearly three centuries the Emperors had without interruption been chosen. Ever since the Peace of Westphalia the Emperor had been little more than the head of a loose confederation of independent sovereigns, many of them very insignificant, who could never be united for any national purpose. All affairs of importance were settled at the diet to which the princes and Free Cities sent their representatives, and what power the Emperor still had in Germany was used for the furtherance of purely Austrian objects.

Austria could never have made head against France in the war but for the steady support she received from England. In fact, throughout the war England rather than Austria appeared as the principal; and one of its most important results was the increased influence that England consequently obtained in Continental affairs.

Another important change in the states-system of Europe was at the same time brought about by the rise of Russia, which, under the rule of Peter the Great, emerged from barbarism and conquered for itself a commanding position in the north-east. The rise of Russia is contemporaneous with the decline of Sweden, at whose expense the aggrandizement of the former was effected.

These were the four great powers—France, Austria, England, and

Russia—but at this period Prussia begins to take place by their side as a fifth. At first, of course, she was not a match for any one of them, but year by year she approached them more nearly as Frederick William added battalion after battalion to his well-organized army. Throughout his reign Prussia seems, as it were, to be unconsciously preparing for the great struggle which lay before her, and which, owing to the consummate skill and resolution of Frederick the Great, ended in her recognition as an equal of the other four powers.

The Peace of Utrecht was not a satisfactory settlement of affairs. Many elements of discord remained outstanding, and others soon began to crop up. To begin with, the peace had failed to reconcile the Emperor and the King of Spain, for while Charles refused to recognise Philip as the rightful king of that country, Philip could not bring himself to acquiesce in the loss of the provinces which had been adjudged to the Emperor. Moreover, Philip was bent on securing for a younger son the reversion of the duchies of Parma, Piacenza and Tuscany, and this the Emperor as feudal superior of the duchies was indisposed to grant.

Then Spain had a grudge against England on the score of Gibraltar and Minorca, and showed it by openly countenancing the Pretender even after his unsuccessful attempt in 1715. To increase the complication, the Emperor managed to offend his allies, England and Holland, by founding a company at Ostend for the purpose of trading with the East Indies. The commercial jealousy of the English and Dutch was aroused, and they protested vehemently that Charles was violating the conditions on which the Netherlands had been assigned to him.

Lastly, a far more serious source of danger lay in the possible extinction of the male line of the House of Hapsburg. Charles VI. was the last male of his house, and, though lie had been married some time, he had only daughters. There had been a son, but he had died in infancy. It was feared that there might be a war of the Austrian Succession, as there had been one of the Spanish. The Emperor drew up a Pragmatic Sanction, a document of a very solemn and formal nature, settling all his vast hereditary possessions on his eldest daughter, Maria Theresa, in default of heirs male. It was, however, extremely probable that the validity of this document might be contested by interested parties, unless it could be placed under the protection of Europe, and the Emperor's whole policy was for many years directed to procuring guarantees for it from every European power.

A vague feeling of uneasiness pervaded Europe, and it was decided that a congress should be held to settle everything. A congress was accordingly held at Cambrai, but, in the midst of its tedious and protracted deliberations, the world was startled by hearing that Spain and Austria had come to a private understanding. All at once the old dread of Austria revived, the fear lest, leagued in close friendship with Spain, she should regain the ascendancy in Europe which she had enjoyed two centuries before. The balance of power was supposed to be in danger, and England, France and Prussia united in a defensive alliance, known as the Alliance of Hanover, (September 3, 1725).

The King of Prussia was won over by the promise of France and England to guarantee his succession to Juliers and Berg. Juliers and Berg, it will be remembered, formed part of the Cleves inheritance, which was divided between Brandenburg and Neuburg, with the stipulation that if male issue failed to either house, the other should inherit the whole. This contingency seemed now likely to occur in the case of Neuburg, and it was known that the Elector Palatine, the representative of the Neuburg line, wished to bequeath the duchies to the Sulzbach branch of his house.

Against the alliance of Hanover the Emperor would of course have been powerless had he not succeeded in detaching the King of Prussia from it, a stroke of policy which proved easier might have been expected. The king had hardly consented to the alliance before he began to repent of the precipitation with which he had acted. Though he had often been slighted and insulted by the Emperor, he remained ardently loyal to the Empire, and felt uneasy at having joined with its natural enemies the French. He feared that he was being drawn into wide schemes which he would not be able to control, and that he might have to fight for objects in which he had no interest.

The balance of power was indeed of vital importance to him, more so than to either England or France; but he had no commerce to suffer from the rivalry of the Ostend Company, nor did it matter to him whether Spain or England held Gibraltar. He suspected that England and France were aiming at the destruction of Austria, and a partition of her dominions, a prospect that filled him with horror. Nor could it escape his penetration that, in the event of war breaking out, he would have to bear the chief brunt of it England was protected by the sea, France by fortresses, but his territories lay exposed to the ravages of Austrian armies.

With thoughts like these in his mind Frederick William sat smoking his pipe one evening in his Tobacco Parliament, as he called the little assemblage of chosen friends whom he used to gather round him when the work, of the day was over. Looking out from the window, he saw his old friend Count von Seckendorf crossing the esplanade in front of the palace. Seckendorf was a general in the Austrian service whose acquaintance he had made in the Spanish Succession war. It was not mere chance that had brought him to Berlin. He was ostensibly passing through on his way to Denmark to transact business there but his real business was with Frederick William, to whom he had been sent by the Austrian Court to cajole him into abandoning his allies.

Seckendorf was an agreeable talker and a pleasant companion, and he soon insinuated himself into the confidence of the simple-minded king, over whom for seven years he exercised an almost unbounded influence. His efforts were seconded by General von Grumbkow, one of Frederick William's most trusted advisers, and a constant attendant at the Tobacco Parliament, who nevertheless allowed himself to be seduced by a pension from Austria. Frederick William became a mere puppet whose strings were held at Vienna.

The immediate result of Seckendorf's machinations was the Treaty of Wusterhausen, (October 12, 1726), by which the King of Prussia agreed to abandon the alliance of Hanover, and to support the Emperor if he should be attacked in Germany. He also guaranteed the Pragmatic Sanction on condition of receiving a guarantee for his own succession to Juliers and Berg, or at any rate to Berg. The Emperor readily gave the required promise, though he had already bound himself to the Elector *Palatine*.

After much diplomacy and some little fighting, most of the difficulties which had agitated Europe since the Peace of Utrecht were disposed of by the Treaty of Treaty of Vienna, (March 16, 1731). England and Holland guaranteed the Pragmatic Sanction, while the Emperor consented to abolish the Ostend Company, and to admit Spanish garrisons into the fortresses of Parma and Piacenza. The active co-operation of the King of Prussia enabled him to obtain a similar guarantee from the diet of the Empire, though the Electors of Bavaria and Saxony protested against it because they had claims on some of the Austrian territories. The Elector *Palatine* protested also, because he suspected that the double-dealing Emperor had guaranteed Juliers and Berg to Prussia. France was now the only power of importance that refused to consent to the Pragmatic Sanction, Spain and Russia having recognised it sometime before.

§3. FATHER AND SON.

While the balance of power in Europe was being laboriously adjusted, the Court of Berlin was distracted by the most violent dissensions, ending at last in an open breach between the king and his eldest son, the crown Prince Frederick, known afterwards as Frederick the Great.

The youth of this prince was passed amid surroundings of singular unpleasantness. The imperious will and ungovernable temper of Frederick William rendered him an object of dread and hatred to his family, and the gloomy severity of his religious views cast a dark shadow over their lives. His rude, uncultivated nature banished refinement from the Court, while his economical habits, degenerating into sordid parsimony when applied to the arrangements of his own household, divested it of everything approaching to luxury. Even the food set upon the royal table was often too nauseous to be eaten.

Frederick William purposed to bring up his eldest son as an exact copy of himself. In his seventh year the prince was taken from the hands of the women and placed under the care of tutors, the mode in which he was to spend his days being exactly prescribed by the king. Very little, time was left for amusement of any kind, and by way of making him hardy he was even stinted in his food and sleep. His education was to comprise only such things as were practically useful. Latin was strictly forbidden, and of French and German he was to learn only so much as would enable him to express himself with fluency.

Endowed by nature with an acute and refined mind, it is not surprising that Frederick revolted from the narrow groove into which his father attempted to force him. He soon became disgusted with the incessant round of drills and reviews to which he was subjected, and he took no pleasure in the great hunting-parties which were the king's favourite recreation. Beer and tobacco, his father's invariable evening solace, were alike odious to him. On the other hand he developed at an early age a taste for literature and music, which was only intensified by the violent efforts made to suppress it. One of his most heinous sins was playing the flute, which to Frederick William appeared a sign of shocking effeminacy. "Fritz," he said with infinite contempt, "Fritz is a fiddler and a poet and will spoil all my labour."

Tyranny on one side produced disobedience on the other, and various causes helped to widen the breach between father and son. The king got to detest his heir, and showed his detestation on every possible occasion. Once he seized him by the hair, dragged him to the window, and would have strangled him with a cord of the curtain had he not been prevented by a chamberlain. Even in public he treated him with the greatest indignity, and would then taunt him with cowardice for not resenting the affronts.

Frederick's position became intolerable, and he resolved to escape from it by flight. The attempt was made at a village near Frankfort, on the occasion of a journey through the Empire on which he accompanied the king, (August 4, 1730). Frederick was then in his nineteenth year. The attempt failed, and the prince lay at the mercy of his enraged father. His crime was aggravated in the king's eyes by the fact of his being an officer in the Prussian army. He was therefore guilty of desertion and the punishment of desertion was death. He was thrown into prison in the fortress of Cüstrin, where he was treated with brutal severity, while his fate and that of his accomplice, Lieutenant von Katte, were being decided by a court-martial.

Katte was condemned to imprisonment for life in a fortress; but this sentence was too lenient to satisfy the savage monarch, so he altered it to death, and caused Katte to be executed before the window of the room in which his son was confined. The court then, after protesting its incompetence to try such a case, sentenced the prince to death, two only of its members being in favour of mercy. Whether the king ever really intended to execute this sentence, it is impossible to say; but those who knew him best feared the worst. Such of the European sovereigns as were on friendly terms with him implored him not to stain his hands with so unnatural a crime, and their entreaties were seconded by the remonstrances of his generals. At last he relented, saying himself that the Emperor's letter had turned the scale; but it was more than a year after his attempted flight before he saw his son, and a partial reconciliation was effected.

The prince's character had been formed and hardened by his sufferings. He had grown from a boy into a man, proud, reserved, and capable of deep dissimulation. He saw the necessity for conforming, outwardly at least, to the will of the king, whose favour he gained by applying himself diligently to the affairs entrusted to his management. Gradually, too, he came to perceive the good qualities which lay underneath the rugged exterior of his father, who, in his turn, recognized with pleasure the abilities of his son. The prince now obtained a separate establishment, and married soon afterwards the Princess Elizabeth Christine of Brunswick Bevern, whom the king had selected for him. From this time he enjoyed a larger measure of liberty than had hitherto been allotted to him—his main reason for consenting to the marriage; so that he could without hindrance cultivate his literary and artistic tastes in the society of friends of his own choice.

§4. THE POLISH ELECTION WAR, AND THE CLOSE OF FREDERICK WILLIAM'S REIGN.

The treaty of Vienna had not been signed much more than two years before a great war broke out. Its cause was the election of a King of Poland, always a source of danger to Europe, owing to the intrigues and jealousies of the neighbouring powers.

Poland was an aristocratic republic, or, as it has been well put, "a democracy of nobles" with an elective king possessing a mere shadow of power. In 1697 the nobles had chosen the Elector of Saxony, who became king with the title of Augustus II., but was driven out some years afterwards by Charles XII. of Sweden, who set up in his stead a Polish nobleman called Stanislaus Lesczinsky. Stanislaus in his turn was expelled by Russian influence, and Augustus remained king for the rest of his life. Nothing more would in all probability have been heard of Stanislaus had not Louis XV. married his daughter, whereby he found a powerful protector.

In 1733 Augustus II. died, and the Polish nobles, bribed by French gold, and assured, as they thought, of French support, proceeded to elect Stanislaus, though aware that they thereby incurred the hostility of Russia and Austria, both of these powers being jealous of French interference in Poland.

Ten days after the election Stanislaus arrived in Warsaw, but was almost immediately expelled by a Russian army under Marshal Lacy, and compelled to take refuge in the fortress of Dantzig. Lacy then caused a faction of the Polish nobles to elect the late king's son, Augustus, Elector of Saxony.

Austria took no part in the election, but it was notorious that she favoured the Saxon candidate, who had gained the Emperor by agreeing to recognise the Pragmatic Sanction, to which his father had always refused to consent.

France then declared war on the Emperor; but, instead of burdening herself with the reinstatement of Stanislaus, she marched an army into Lorraine. The conquest of this province was, in fact, her motive for meddling in the Polish election, and she had shown great astuteness in making the election a *casus belli*, for it was a matter as to which

England and Holland were indifferent, and therefore unlikely to support the Emperor. Spain and Sardinia joined with the spoiler and attacked the Austrian dominions in Italy.

It is obvious that it now became a matter of importance for Austria to secure the friendship of Prussia. When France declared war, Frederick William, though personally inclined to favour Stanislaus, offered to support the Emperor on the Rhine with 30,000 or 40,000 men. Such, however, was the infatuation of Austria that she refused this handsome offer from jealousy of the rising power of Prussia, and curtly demanded the contingent of 10,000 which Frederick William was bound by treaty to supply.

The king was bitterly mortified by the refusal and by the studied neglect and contempt of the Austrian Court, which persisted in regarding him as a subject and an inferior. But he was not yet prepared to throw himself into the arms of France, for, apart from the consideration that he would thereby lose the Imperial guarantee of Juliers and Berg, he was too mindful of his position as a prince of the Empire to join with a power engaged in dismembering it. Moreover, he had more regard for treaties than was common at that time. Yet the situation was one from which his more clear-headed and less scrupulous son would assuredly have found means to extract some advantage for Prussia.

In June, 1734, Dantzig capitulated, but Stanislaus made his escape into Prussian territory, whereupon the Emperor demanded that he should be given up to the Russians. Frederick William indignantly refused to do anything of the kind; nor was he more disposed to compliance when Charles went on to demand the dismissal of the French ambassador from Berlin because the Empire was at war with France. The Polish war marks a stage in the transition already alluded to.

The demeanour of Austria was forcing Frederick William to break loose from his, old habit of considering every question from the point of view of a prince of the Empire. More and more he came to look upon Prussia as an independent power, though he was never able to bring himself to any definite act of self-assertion.

The war ended in the utter discomfiture of the Emperor, who had to surrender Naples and Sicily to Don Carlos (the second son of the King of Spain), and a portion of Lombardy to Sardinia. Augustus remained King of Poland, and Stanislaus, whose rights were quietly passed over, though he was permitted to retain the empty title of royalty, was compensated by receiving for life the duchies of Lorraine and Bar. After his death they were to pass to France. The Duke of Lorraine, on whom the Emperor intended to confer the hand of Maria Theresa, obtained the reversion of Tuscany in compensation for the loss of his hereditary dominions, the Grand-duke of Tuscany, the last of the Medici, being at the point of death and without heirs. Parma and Piacenza reverted to the Emperor. Finally, France agreed to guarantee the Pragmatic Sanction.

As Frederick William's life drew to a close he experienced more and more the ill-will of the Austrian Court. Satisfied at last that it was not, and perhaps never had been, in earnest about Juliers and Berg, he had the mortification of feeling that the devotion of a lifetime had been thrown away. One consolation alone remained to him. Pointing to his son, with whom he was now completely reconciled, he said with pride and sorrow, "There stands one who will avenge me."

CHAPTER 4

Frederick the Great and the First Silesian War

§1. ACCESSION AND CHARACTER OF FREDERICK.

Frederick was born on January 24, 1712, and became king on May 31, 1740. In personal appearance he was rather good-looking than otherwise, well-made, though below the average height, and inclined to stoutness. He had the fair hair and blue eyes of the North Germans, regular and delicate features, and a face with great power of expression.

At the time of his accession he was little known except to a few intimate friends, and even these had no idea what manner of man he really was. For some years past he had lived for the most part in retirement at Reinsberg, a palace erected under his own supervision on an estate purchased for him by his father. There, surrounded by friends of his own choosing, many of them foreigners, he led a careless convivial life, seemingly engrossed in the pleasures of society, literature, art, music, and the table. No one knew that while amusing himself with concerts and private theatricals, while writing French verses and corresponding with Voltaire, he was applying himself indefatigably to military and political affairs, and acquiring a great aptitude for business. No one suspected that beneath the easy-going, intellectual voluptuary there lay concealed a stern, self-willed, ambitious despot.

During the last year at Reinsberg he had been preparing for publication a refutation of Machiavelli's *Prince*. The *Anti-Machiavel*, as the work was called, contained an elaborate statement of Frederick's notions of what a king should be, and an indignant declamation against ambition, conquest, arbitrary government, and so on. It was published in the autumn of 1740, anonymously, but the authorship was no secret. By the irony of fate it had hardly been published two months before its author was engaged in a war of which ambition was the avowed motive.

Men thought that his accession would usher in a golden age of peace and plenty under the beneficent sway of a philosopher-king, whose sole care would be the happiness of his subjects, and whose attention would be directed, not to the preparation for war, but to the cultivation and encouragement of the arts and sciences. The illusion quickly vanished, though some of the young king's earliest acts were calculated to confirm it. Men of eminence in science and literature were invited to Berlin, and Maupertuis, the great French mathematician, was requested to preside over an academy that was shortly to be refounded in the Prussian capital. Within the first few days of his reign, Frederick abolished legal torture except in a few specified cases, granted complete freedom to the press, and declared himself in favour of universal toleration in religion, in all which matters he was far in advance of his age.

He further gave his ministers to understand that he regarded his own interests and those of his people as identical, but that he wished the preference to be given to the latter if ever the two should seem to be incompatible. This declaration was followed by a liberal distribution of corn from the public granaries at moderate rates to the poor of several famine-stricken provinces. Next came the disbandment of the useless and costly regiment of Potsdam giants, which appeared for the last time at Frederick William's funeral, a measure which gave some countenance to the rumour that the army was going to be reduced.

Yet Frederick soon showed that he meant to rule with the strong hand, as his father had ruled before him. His reforms were merely superficial, and did not touch the fabric of government bequeathed to him by the late king. In this no alteration of any importance was made, except that Frederick took the reins into his own hands far more completely than Frederick William had ever done.

The power of the sovereign was immense in Prussia. There was perhaps no country in Europe where the crown was, on the one hand, less overshadowed by great nobles or ecclesiastics, and, on the other, less limited by popular rights, none which offered such facilities for absolutism to a strong-willed and ambitious prince. The Prussian nobility was very powerful; but it was not powerful against the sovereign. Its privileges were enormous, and Frederick, an intense aristocrat at heart, in spite of his talk about equality, preserved them in their integrity. But it had within its ranks no great families of historical reputation, standing close round the throne, as in the ancient monarchies of Europe, and exercising upon it an undefined influence. Nor, again, though each province had its own local administration, was there any general assembly of the whole nation which could place a check on the crown. The Prussian monarchy was in fact, as might be expected from its origin, a compound of separate units welded into a strong centralized state by a century of military despotism.

Frederick saw the strength of his position, and availed himself of it to the utmost. When Prince Leopold of Anhalt-Dessau expressed a hope that he and his sons might be allowed to retain the offices and authority they had enjoyed in the late reign, he replied that they should certainly be continued in their offices, but that he knew of no authority save that which resided in the king. Far from intending to reduce the army, he increased it by 16,000 men. The strict economy of the late reign was in no wise relaxed, though Frederick's common sense prevented it from degenerating into the ridiculous parsimony which had made his father's court the laughing stock of Europe. It was soon remarked that Frederick as king showed no resentment towards those who had treated him with harshness in the days when as crown prince be was out of favour with his father.

Nor, on the other hand, did he manifest any undue partiality for the friends of his youth, by promoting them to places for which they were unfit. Neither present affection nor gratitude for the past had the least weight with him against the public advantage. Almost all of Frederick William's ministers were left in their posts, though with diminished power and influence. Frederick's ministers were little more than clerks. He kept all power in his own hands, and superintended every department with the keenest vigilance and with untiring energy. This system of supervision or interference was carried a great deal too far. Frederick did all manner of things himself which might have been done as well or better by subordinates, and, if his constitution had not been a very strong one, he must have broken down under the weight of the immense mass of business which he transacted daily. When it passed into weaker hands, the system collapsed.

Frederick possessed a large share of the qualities which make a great ruler: a strong love of order, a, very clear insight into men and things, great administrative capacities, combined with indefatigable industry, and a mind capable of forming the most extensive schemes and of attending at the same time to the minutest details of their execution. To these qualities must be added a rare strength of will and a self-reliance that never faltered.

His system of government was doubtless despotic and paternal, at times even tyrannical; but for a young country that has to fight for its existence, a paternal despotism is no bad thing, at any rate when the despot identifies himself with its welfare so completely as Frederick did. It may be questioned whether under any other form of government Prussia could have weathered the storms of the Seven Years' War.

Nor should it be forgotten that under the shadow of this despotism an unparalleled freedom of speech was permitted. The liberty of the press which Frederick granted at the commencement of his reign was no mere empty form. Satires on the king were published in Berlin which would not have been endured in any other capital in Europe. "My people and I," he said, "have come to an agreement which satisfies us both. They are to say what they please, and I am to do what I please." The understanding was well observed on both sides. Conscious of strength and conscious of possessing the love and esteem of the mass of his subjects, Frederick looked down with serene indifference on all that his enemies might say of him.

One day as he rode through Berlin, he saw a crowd of people staring up at something on the wail, and on sending his groom to inquire what it was, found it to be a caricature of himself. The placard was put so high that it was difficult to read it, so Frederick ordered it to be placed lower, in order that the people might not have to stretch out their necks. The words were hardly spoken, when with a joyous shout the placard was pulled down and torn into a thousand pieces, while a hearty cheer followed the king as he rode away.

Frederick was a great administrator, but he was something more. He was the most clear-sighted statesman in Europe. What strikes one most about his policy is its definiteness, and the limitation of his aims to what was practically attainable. He never let himself drift. He always knew what he wanted, and he generally knew how to get it. If he was not very scrupulous about the means he employed, he must be judged by the standard of the age in which he lived, and that standard was not a high one. The skill displayed in the formation of his plans was not more conspicuous than the vigour and rapidity with which they were executed when the proper moment had arrived. When he had made up his mind to strike, he struck at once and with decision.

Equally remarkable were the calmness of his judgment and the power he possessed of taking an unbiased survey of any situation in which he found himself. Not elated with victory, not disheartened by adversity, he knew how to use the one with moderation and to bear the other with fortitude.

His fortitude was heroic. It never, except once for a moment, gave way amid disasters that would have crushed any ordinary man. For years during the latter part of the Seven Years' War he must have lived in the full conviction that, do what he would, he could hardly escape destruction. Yet he went on with ever-diminishing resources, day after day devising new expedients, and always showing a bold front to the enemy. And he triumphed at last by the sheer force of his relentless will.

The brilliant military talents for which he was distinguished late in life are a remarkable proof, on the one hand, of great mental powers, on the other, of energy and determination. Frederick had no inborn genius for war. His early campaigns were full of blunders, and owed their success to the excellence of the Prussian troops and to the skill of the Prussian generals. It was simply by dint of hard study and by long pondering over dearly bought experience that he made himself the first commander of his age.

Of Frederick's personal character it is not possible to speak in the terms of admiration that may justly be applied to his character as a ruler. There is indeed, no reason for believing that the charges of gross immorality insinuated against him by certain writers have any foundation in fact. On the contrary, with the exception of some youthful indiscretions, his life appears to have been perfectly pure. But he was not a man to inspire those about him with love and devotion. That he was capable of deep feeling there is no doubt, but he very seldom showed it. He was cold, haughty, and reserved. His nature seems to have been soured by the brutal treatment he endured in his boyhood. Originally gentle and lovable, it became hard and selfish. He possessed the dangerous gift of sarcasm, and he used it without mercy Yet when he wished to make himself agreeable no one could be more so. His conversational talents and his wit were really considerable, and he had, when he chose to exert it, a rare charm of manner.

With the mass of his subjects Frederick was certainly popular. His sarcasms were not indulged in at their expense. To them and especially to his soldiers he was endeared more and more as his reign went on not more by his exploits, of which they were justly proud, than by his genial affability, by a certain homely simplicity of manner, an aptitude for humorous repartee, and by the good humour with which he often allowed the most astonishing plain-spoken things to be said to himself. Innumerable stories are told of old "Father Fritz," as his soldiers loved to call him, illustrating these traits of his character. One anecdote will suffice as an instance of the extraordinary freedom which common soldiers were sometimes permitted to use in addressing their haughty and imperious sovereign. In the course of the Seven Years' War, a regiment just about to go into winter quarters was suddenly ordered to march against the enemy. Frederick rode by the side of the men as they marched, and overhearing a grenadier cursing and grumbling at the hardness of their fate, said, "Be calm, my children, you shall have all the better winter quarters for it."

"I only hope you're not lying, Fritz," was the unblushing reply.

"No," said the king, good-humouredly, "no, really I'm not; I keep my word."

"Well then,!' exclaimed the grenadier, "now we are ready to drive the devil out of hell."

This particular anecdote may or may not be true, but there are so many of the same kind that it is impossible to believe all to be fictitious.

§2. State of Europe at Fredericks Accession.

The question of Juliers and Berg, which had played so prominent a part in Frederick William's reign, remained unsettled at the time of his death, though the advanced age of the Elector Palatine made it evident that the succession would soon be vacant; Disgusted with the double-dealing of the Emperor, Frederick William had towards the close of his reign applied to France for support in maintaining his rights. His overtures were favourably received, but led to nothing, because France was unwilling to see any stronger power in possession of the important duchies on the Rhine. Moreover, the widespread belief that nothing would induce the Prussian king to go to war deprived him of the consideration that would otherwise have been shown to the master of so many battalions. Frederick, on his accession, sounded both England and France to ascertain how far he might rely on either of them for assistance, but avoided entangling himself in definite alliances, preferring to keep his hands free so that he might act in whatever way seemed most advantageous.

At the time of Frederick's accession the political horizon was tolerably clear. There was war between England and Spain, but that was far away on condition of the Spanish main, and though it was expected that the King of France would before long espouse the cause of his Spanish kinsman, he had not done so as yet. The peace of Europe remained unbroken, and there were no signs of the coming storm.

The Emperor had procured from every state of importance a guarantee of his Pragmatic Sanction; and although Prince Eugene had told him that that the only guarantee worth having was an army of 200,000 men and a full treasury, he fondly hoped that engagements obtained with such difficulty would not be lightly repudiated. There was, moreover, no immediate prospect of the good faith of the guarantors being put to the test. Charles VI. was only fifty-five years old and in the enjoyment of perfect health, so much so that he had not yet abandoned the hope of male issue. For this reason he had deferred getting his son-in-law, Francis of Lorraine, Grand-duke of Tuscany, crowned King of the Romans, which would have ensured his following him as Emperor.

This might easily have been done, and would have been quite in accordance with precedent. For some centuries past the Emperors had usually contrived to get a son or some other near relation crowned King of the Romans in their lifetime, and, when this had been done, the King of the Romans succeeded at once on the Emperor's death, without any farther coronation or election. Charles, however, not wishing to bar the claims of any son that he might still have, hesitated to get the ceremony performed upon his son-in-law, and the result was, that when he died the electors chose another man instead of Francis of Lorraine.

England and France had each for many years been ruled by a single minister. Sir Robert. Walpole had been Prime Minister of England for eighteen years, and Cardinal Fleury had for almost as long a period governed France in the name of Louis XV . Both ministers were distinguished for their pacific policy, yet each was before the close of his career forced into what he believed to be an unjust or impolitic war. In each case the love of power proved stronger than political principles, and the latter were sacrificed that the former might be retained.

The war between England and Spain arose out of the commercial relations of the two countries. English trade with the Spanish colonies was restricted by treaties within very narrow limits, but smuggling went on to such an extent that almost all the commerce of Spanish America was in English hands. Frequent collisions naturally ensued between the English traders and the Spanish coastguards, who claimed to exercise a right of search over English vessels, and public opinion in England was inflamed by reports of atrocities perpetrated on English sailors. The stories were for the most part gross exaggerations, but they were implicitly believed, and produced a marvellous effect. So great was the popular ferment, and so artfully was it stimulated by the opposition leaders, that Walpole, against his better judgment, was driven to declare war, (November 4, 1739).

The near relationship of the Kings of France and Spain made it probable that the latter would not long remain neutral, and it was chiefly the consideration of this risk which made Walpole should join shrink from declaring war. So long as England was at peace, and especially so long as she was at peace with France, there was little if any danger of a Stuart rebellion: the events of 1745-46 are a sufficient justification of Walpole' s policy. The contingency which he dreaded—war with France—occurred, but not until both countries were involved in the great war of the Austrian Succession, which broke out on the unexpected death of the Emperor.

§3. Death of the Emperor and its Results.

Charles VI. died on October 20, 1740, after a very short illness, caused, it is said, by eating a dish of mushrooms. In accordance with the Pragmatic Charles VI. Sanction, his eldest daughter, Maria Theresa, was proclaimed Archduchess of Austria, Queen of Hungary, Queen of Bohemia, and under various titles sovereign of all the lands that had owned her father as their lord. She was not yet twenty-four years old when the untimely death of her father suddenly called her to a position as perilous as it was exalted. But young as she was she showed herself fully equal to the emergency, and her own high spirit inspired all about her with enthusiasm. She was strikingly handsome, and she combined a most fascinating manner with a powerful and masculine understanding. Her energy and determination never flagged, and her courage seemed always to rise in proportion to the difficulties she had to contend with. She was a very noble-minded woman, animated by deep religious principles and by a strong sense of duty. Later on in life her religious zeal too often took the form of bigotry and intolerance, and, as was the case with Frederick too, her love of power and influence led her to exercise an inquisitorial scrutiny over the private affairs of her subjects.

And yet, however, these faults were not apparent. In all respects she was a worthy antagonist for the great Frederick, her almost lifelong foe. It is said that at one time he wished to marry her; but, apart from the difference of religion, the pride of the Austrian Court and the predilection of Maria Theresa herself for Francis of Lorraine were insuperable objections to a marriage which would have altered the whole course of German and European history.

Charles was hardly dead before the validity of the Pragmatic Sanction was contested. A Bavarian envoy was already on the road to Vienna when the tidings of his decease reached Munich. The envoy had been despatched on the 21st, in anticipation of the event, to protest against the accession of Maria Theresa in the name of Charles Albert, Elector of Bavaria, and to assert the Bavarian claims to a large portion of the Austrian dominions. The elector was descended from the Archduchess Anne, eldest daughter of the Emperor Ferdinand I., who died in 1564, and his claims rested on the will of Ferdinand, of which there was a copy at Munich. The elector maintained that Ferdinand had settled his dominions on his daughter Anne and her descendants in the event of failure of his own heirs male, and the Bavarian ambassador at Vienna was instructed to demand the production of the will. The will was produced, and to the ambassador's amazement was found to contain the words "lawfully begotten (*eheliche*) descendants" instead of "male (*männliche*) descendants." Whether the copy was incorrect or the will itself had been tampered with nobody knows, but it is tolerably certain that Charles Albert himself believed in the justice of his claims.

Meanwhile a far more dangerous enemy than the elector was silently preparing for action. Frederick of Prussia saw in the Emperor's death an opportunity for aggrandizement such as might never occur again, and with characteristic promptitude determined at once to utilize it by seizing Silesia and reviving his determines claims on the duchies of Jägerndorf, Liegnitz, Brieg, and Wohlau. Having formed this resolution, he sent for Podewils and Schwerin, the most trusted of his ministers and his best general, to consult with them as to the mode of executing it. The seizure itself would not be difficult; the real difficulties would come afterwards.

After four days' deliberation it was decided, to begin by taking possession of Silesia, peaceable possession if possible, and then to open negotiations with Maria Theresa. The usual practice of the Hohenzollerns had been to offer their services to Austria, and to trust to her promises for obtaining what they wanted in return. The futility of this mode of procedure had been made apparent in the case of Frederick William. Austria accepted his services and then broke her promises. Frederick determined to get his reward first and give her no opportunity for perfidy.

The terms he was prepared to offer were the following: to defend Austria against all other claimants; to assist the Grand-duke of Tuscany in obtaining the Imperial Crown; to resign the Prussian claims on Juliers and Berg; and to advance a considerable sum of ready money. In return he demanded the whole or at any rate part of Silesia. It required some effrontery to offer such terms to the haughty Austrian, and Frederick had small hope of their being accepted, but he thought it advisable to proceed thus instead of at once taking up an attitude of irreconcilable hostility, and claiming the four duchies as his right. The propositions were not presented at Vienna until he had already entered Silesia at the head of his army.

The question whether the seizure of Silesia was or was not justifiable is one on which the most divergent opinions have been, and are still, entertained. It looks on the face of it like a flagrant violation of the law of nations, and Frederick admits himself that the desire of making himself a name was at any rate one of his motives. There are, however, considerations that may be urged in extenuation of his conduct. His father had guaranteed the Pragmatic Sanction, but his guarantee was conditional on the Emperor's promise to secure to him the succession to Juliers and Berg. Yet so far was Charles from doing this that he actually agreed to allow to the other claimant provisional possession of the duchies. Again, the contention that the peace of Europe would have been preserved if Frederick had kept quiet, has little to justify it. Apart from the probable contingency of the war between England and Spain spreading, there was the fact that the Elector of Bavaria had already asserted his claims to Austrian territories, and that France had already determined to back him.

Within ten days of the Emperor's death, Cardinal Fleury said to the Prussian ambassador that France had given her guarantee to the Pragmatic Sanction, subject to the clause 'saving the rights of a third party, a reservation' which, as the ambassador observed, annihilated the guarantee altogether. Moreover, Saxony had claims, too, and if Bavaria moved in the matter, Saxony would move also, and it was almost certain that she would try to obtain that very Silesia over which the Hohenzollerns had ancient rights. As to these Silesian claims, Frederick does not say much, though he alludes to them in his *Histoi de mon*

Temps as being incontestable. They were certainly valid in themselves; their weak point was length of time they had lain dormant.

Less excusable than the actual seizure of Silesia was the manner in which it was done; the perfidy with which Frederick concealed his intentions under the mask of friendship; the hypocrisy with which, when his army was occupying Silesia, he pretended to be acting in the interests of Maria Theresa.

It may be asked why, if Frederick wanted to seize something, he did not seize Juliers and Berg, where there was no manner of doubt about the justice of his claims. The answer is not far to seek. By occupying the Rhine duchies he would have offended France as well as Austria, whereas France would not care a straw about his aggrandizing himself on the Oder. Then, again, Juliers and Berg were far away, Silesia was close at home, contiguous to the main body of his dominions, and in every respect a more valuable acquisition.

§4. The Conquest of Silesia.

On December 16, 1740, Frederick entered Silesia at the head of 28,000 men, averring that he came with no hostile intentions against Austria, but merely to guard his own interests there in the troubled times he saw coming. On hearing of his preparations, the Austrians had got together a force of 7000 men, which, though unable to keep the field, was sufficient to garrison the fortresses. Three of these, Glogau, Brieg, and Neisse, were strong places, and it was hoped that they would be able to hold out till the spring, when they would be relieved by an Austrian army, especially as a severe frost set in before the close of the year and rendered siege operations impossible.

Except from the fortresses, Frederick met with no resistance. The inhabitants were either indifferent or well disposed to his cause. Two-thirds of them were Protestants, and these welcomed him as the champion of Protestantism coming from the north, as Charles XII. of Sweden had come before, to secure to them the right of worshipping God as they pleased. Of course Frederick had no idea of stirring up a religious war. Such a thing would have been utterly foreign to his nature. He merely announced that, as in his own dominions, so in Silesia all forms of religion were to be protected. But to men who had been oppressed and persecuted for their religion, as the Silesian Protestants had been, even toleration and equality might well seem a welcome boon.

Before the end of January, Frederick had made himself master of

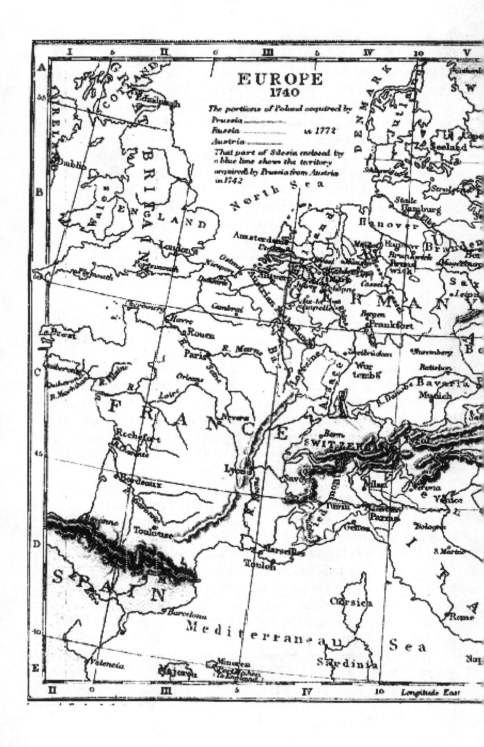

EUROPE
1740

The portions of Poland acquired by
Prussia
Russia —————— in 1772
Austria
That part of Silesia enclosed by
a blue line shows the territory
acquired by Prussia from Austria
in 1742

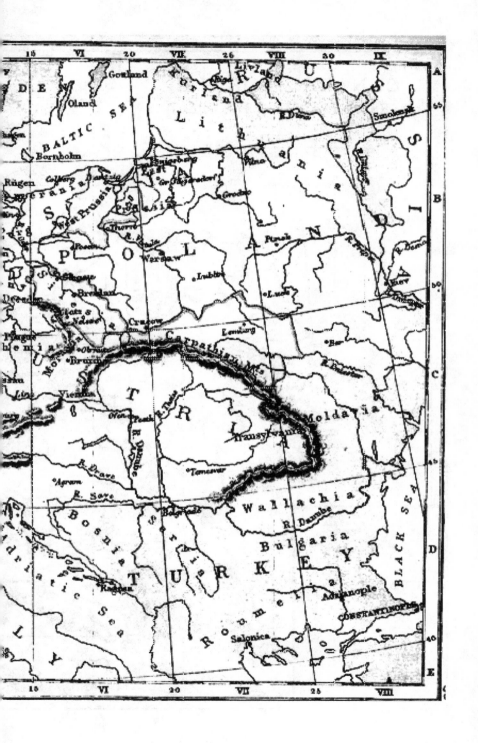

CENTRAL EUROPE
WARS OF FREDERICK THE GREAT

English Miles

NETHERLANDS

UNITED

Hanover

Stade

Ratseven

R. Aller

Hastenbeck

Lutternberg

Hesse Cassel

Cadsam
Orland Sluys
Nieuport
Furnes S.
Ypres
Lille
Tournay
Menin

Ghent
Malines
Antwerp
Bruges
Louvain
Brussels

Maestricht
Jülich
Aix la Chapelle
Liège

Netherlands

Frankfort
Hanau
Dettingen
Aschaffenb

Rothenburg

Gemersheim

Lorraine

Meuse

Alsace

Strasburg

Würtemberg

COMPLETION OF PRUSSIA
On same scale

Memel

Königsberg R. Pregel

Stallupönen

Gross-Jägerndorf

East Prussia

SWITZERLAND

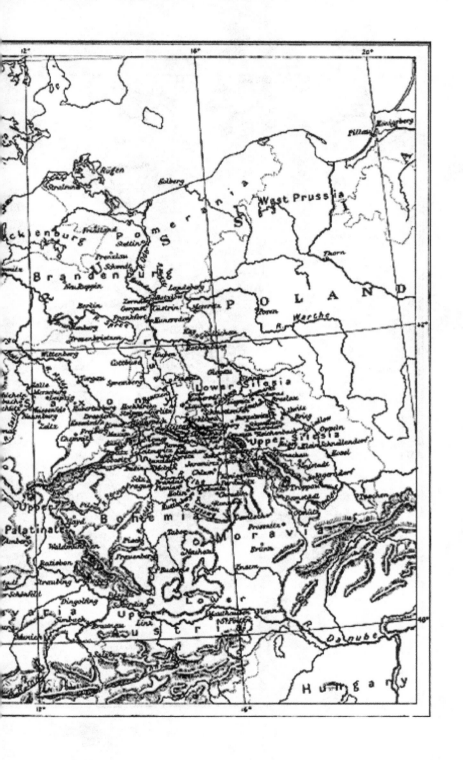

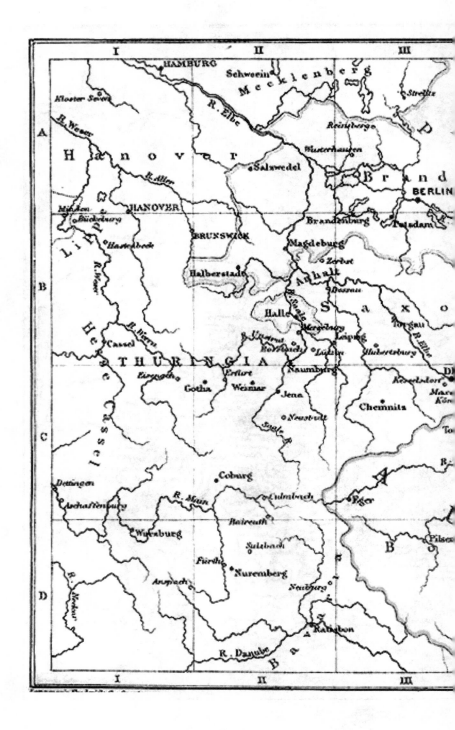

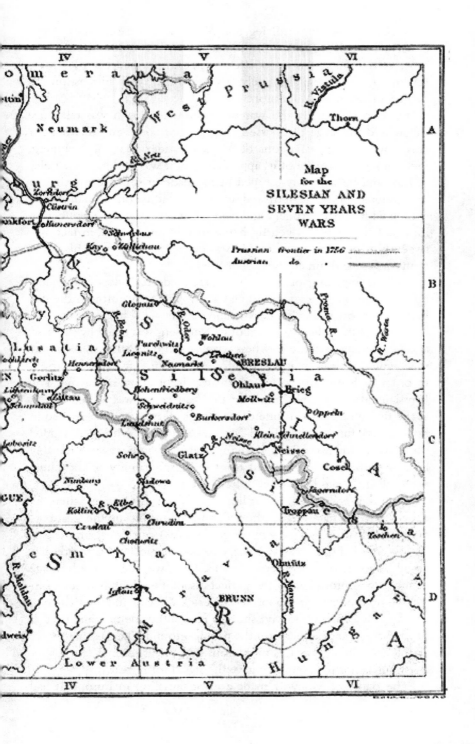

Map
for the
SILESIAN AND
SEVEN YEARS
WARS

Prussian frontier in 1756 ————
Austrian do. ————

all Silesia except Glogau, Brieg, and Neisse, and these fortresses were closely blockaded. Breslau the capital opened its gates after a mere show of resistance. His negotiations with Austria had been less successful. Maria Theresa absolutely refused to treat with him as long as he had a man in her dominions.

Early in the spring the war was resumed. Glogau was taken by storm, and the siege of Neisse had just been commenced, when an Austrian army appeared out of Moravia under Marshal Neipperg. Frederick was unaware of its approach until it was within a few miles of him, and he narrowly escaped being made prisoner. Gathering in his scattered posts, he retreated with all rapidity on Ohlau, which contained his heavy artillery and stores. But the Austrians were before him, and succeeded in getting between him and Ohlau, in fact, between him and Brandenburg. He was entirely cut off from his communications, and forced to risk a battle.

On the morning of April 10, 1741, Frederick advanced against the Austrians as they lay encamped at Mollwitz. All through the day before the snow had fallen heavily, and neither army had any very distinct idea of the other's whereabouts. Neipperg was taken by surprise, and but for the extreme slowness with which the Prussians manoeuvred, would have been attacked before he had time to form his troops in order of battle. But at first the battle went all in his favour. The Prussian cavalry was no match for the Austrian; it was routed almost at the first onset, and, in spite of the king's efforts to rally it, it fled in hopeless confusion. Then Field-Marshal Schwerin, who commanded the Prussian infantry, either thinking that the battle was irretrievably lost, or wishing to be relieved from the responsibility of the king's presence, implored him to retire from the field.

Frederick consented, and galloped off towards Oppeln, where he expected to be able to cross the Oder. In the meantime the steadfastness of the Prussian infantry retrieved the day. Again and again the gallant Römer led the Austrian cavalry to the charge, but no impression could be made on those serried ranks. Then was seen the advantage of the iron ramrods and of the perfect discipline which had been impressed on the Prussian troops by Frederick William and the Prince of Dessau. The Prussians got five shots to two of the enemy's, and fired as steadily as if they had been on the parade-ground. The Austrians were unable to stand against this murderous fire, and at seven o'clock, after five hours' fighting, Neipperg gave the signal for retreat.

The Battle of Mollwitz made a great sensation in Europe. It had never been supposed that the untried troops of Prussia could resist the veterans of Austria, Louis XV., when he heard of Frederick's invasion of Silesia, said, "The man is mad." But Mollwitz showed that the man was not mad, and that a new power had arisen in Europe. Frederick's camp was sought by envoys from almost every court in Europe, and amongst them, on the part of France, came Marshal Belleisle.

Belleisle was a man of brilliant talents and boundless ambition. His mind was full of the wildest schemes for the aggrandisement of France, and his imagination soared over every obstacle that lay in his path. His daring projects fascinated even the dull soul of Louis XV. When the Battle of Mollwitz was fought, he was making a tour in regal splendour through the German courts, with the object of preventing the Grand-duke of Tuscany from being chosen Emperor. He had not quite decided on whom the perilous honour was to be conferred, but the Elector of Bavaria was his favourite candidate. He saw in the difficulties of the House of Hapsburg an opportunity for the total destruction of its power. He projected the formation of a grand alliance against Austria under the leadership of France, which should embrace Spain, Prussia, Bavaria, and perhaps Sweden and Saxony. Already he looked upon the Queen of Hungary as vanquished, and imagined himself dividing her dominions as he pleased.

"He talked," said Frederick, "as if all her provinces were up at auction." The French were to get the Austrian Netherlands, and Germany was to be cut up into four little kingdoms, which France, the arbiter of Europe, might play off one against the other as she pleased.

Frederick was not at all attracted by Belleisle's programme. He had no wish to pull down Austria in order to set up France in her place, Yet, situated as he was, it was very difficult for him to refuse the French alliance. He was fully alive to the danger of accepting it. The French might use him as a tool, and then desert him, as they had deserted Stanislaus in his Polish war. To accept it would be a wide departure from the traditional policy of his house, but he could hardly dispense with French assistance unless he could make an accommodation with Austria. Austria herself was a power of vast resources, if she only knew how to use them, and it was not yet certain that several of the guarantors of the Pragmatic Sanction would hot come to her rescue. England, he knew, would stand by her. She had already supplied the money with which Neipperg's army was equipped.

Fearing that he might be attacked by a coalition, Frederick was eagerly desirous of an honourable peace with Austria. His terms were

PRUSSIAN ARMY DURING BATTLE OF MOLLWITZ 1741

studiously moderate. He would be content with Lower Silesia and Breslau, the same that he would have taken before Mollwitz. His efforts were, however, in vain, though seconded by England, who was anxious to restore harmony between the two German powers and to unite them against France. The Court of Vienna, blind to or regardless of the dangers that surrounded it, refused to conciliate this dangerous enemy, who might at that time have been converted into a staunch friend. Relying on Cardinal Fleury's known aversion to war, the Austrian ministers still cherished the belief that France would adhere to her guarantee.

When all hopes of a satisfactory peace with Austria had been exhausted, Frederick entered into a defensive alliance with France, (June 5). The terms of the treaty were exceedingly vague. The main points, however, were as follows: France guaranteed Lower Silesia and Breslau to Frederick, and Frederick relinquished his claims on Juliers and Berg, and promised to vote for the Elector of Bavaria as Emperor. At the same time he stipulated that France should without delay send auxiliary troops to the assistance of the elector, and induce Sweden to declare war on Russia to prevent her from succouring the Queen of Hungary.

France now began to act with energy. In the month of August two French armies crossed the Rhine, each about 40,000 strong. The first marched into Westphalia, and frightened George II. into concluding a treaty of neutrality for Hanover, and promising his vote to the Elector of Bavaria. The second advanced through South Germany on Passau, the frontier city of Bavaria and Austria. As soon as it arrived on German soil, the French officers assumed the blue and white cockade of Bavaria, for it was the cue of France, to appear only as an auxiliary, and the nominal command of her army was vested in the elector.

From Passau the French and Bavarians passed into Upper Austria, and on September 11 entered its capital, Linz, where the elector assumed the title of Archduke. Five days later Saxony joined the allies. Sweden had already declared war on Russia. Spain trumped up an old claim and attacked the Austrian dominions in Italy. It seemed as if Belleisle's schemes were about to be crowned with complete success. Had the allies pushed forward, Vienna must have fallen into their hands. But the French did not wish to be too victorious lest they should make the elector too powerful, and so independent of them. Therefore, after six weeks' delay, they turned aside to the conquest of Bohemia.

Breathing time was afforded to Maria Theresa, but her situation was still very critical. As she could not yet resolve to grant terms which would satisfy Frederick, she was obliged to fall back her Hungarian subjects. The Hungarians had usually been rather a source of apprehension than of security to the Austrian monarchy, but Maria Theresa won their loyal support by important concessions. She promised to restore their ancient constitution, which had been abolished by her ancestors, and the Hungarian magnates, touched by the misfortunes of their young and beautiful sovereign, voted with acclamation an insurrection or general arming of the country.

The insurrection would have been of little use to the queen if her enemies had really desired her destruction. She might easily have been overwhelmed before the Hungarians could take the field. But, while the French were holding back for fear of making the Elector of Bavaria too strong, the King of Prussia allowed himself to be detached from his allies. Frederick had been pursuing a very tortuous policy during the summer. In spite of his treaty with France he continued to negotiate with Austria, and on October 9 he met Neipperg at the Castle of Klein Schnellendorf, and agreed to a secret compact. Neipperg was to be allowed to retire unmolested into Moravia, and Neisse was to be delivered to Frederick after a feigned siege. A definite peace was to be concluded before the end of the year. Frederick insisted on the compact being kept a profound secret, and intimated his intention of disavowing it if it should be allowed to transpire.

The compact was of great advantage to Maria Theresa, as it enabled her to concentrate her forces against her remaining enemies. Neipperg, released from Silesia, withdrew into Moravia, where he was joined by the Grand-duke Francis with 30,000 men. The combined Austrian army advanced into Bohemia, and, though too late to save Prague, it was able to prevent any further conquests. The French generalship was very bad. Belleisle ought before this time to have taken command of the allied army, but he was disabled by rheumatic gout, and forced to resign his post into the hands of Marshal Broglie, a very inadequate substitute. The French and Bavarians were shut up in Prague, and cut off from their conquests in Upper Austria, while these were menaced by another Austrian army under Count Khevenhüller.

Khevenhüller retook Linz on January 24, 1742, the very day on which Charles Albert, Elector of Bavaria, was raised to the imperial throne with the title of Charles VII. He had reached the summit of his ambition, and henceforth his fortunes steadily declined. He was head of the Holy Roman Empire, but he was no longer master of his own dominions. While Khevenhüller was reconquering Upper Austria the Hungarian Pandours had burst into Bavaria from the Tyrolese mountains, and were spreading destruction far and wide. Munich fell into their hands (February 13) almost at the very moment when the Emperor was being solemnly crowned at Frankfort. Charles's only hope lay in Frederick, whom he implored to make a diversion in his favour.

Frederick had already determined to interfere. His Silesian conquests were secured by no treaty, and it was becoming apparent that Austria had no intention of concluding one. He began to be alarmed at her successes, and the fact that the compact of Klein Schnellendorf had long since been made public gave him an excuse for resuming hostilities. Early in 1742 he entered Moravia in conjunction with a body of Saxon troops, but the campaign was rendered fruitless by the obstinacy of the Saxon commanders, and when the allies parted it was with feelings of mutual dissatisfaction.

After the departure of the Saxons, Frederick retired into Bohemia, and fell back in the direction of Prague. At Chrudim he heard that an Austrian army was advancing against him, under Prince Charles of Lorraine, Maria Theresa's brother-in-law. A battle was fought at Chotusitz,(May 17), and again the Prussians gained a complete victory. Austria was now ready for peace with Prussia, England had advised it all along, but Maria Theresa would not consent to give up Silesia, 'the fairest jewel of her crown,' until she had tried her fortune in another battle. By the Peace of Breslau, (June 11), she surrendered all Silesia (with the exception of Teschen, Troppau, and Jägerndorf), together with the county of Glatz. The French were very indignant when they heard that their ally had concluded a separate peace, but Frederick had good reason for believing that they would have treated him in the same way if they had had the opportunity.

The Peace of Breslau added to the Prussian kingdom a province which enlarged its area by one-third, and increased its population and revenue by about one-half, a rich and fertile province, full of towns and villages, and one which, by its geographical conditions, no less than on religious grounds, belonged naturally to the northern rather than to the southern German power. From Bohemia and Moravia Silesia was cut off by mountain chains through which the passes were few and difficult; the natural highway of its commerce was the broad stream of the Oder, which traverses the country from end to end before passing through the plains of Brandenburg on its way to the Baltic.

The ease with which the conquest of Silesia was effected, and the loyalty with which its inhabitants held fast to Prussia during the Seven Years' War, show that the transfer of allegiance gave no violent shock to their feelings, and indicate a consciousness on their part that destiny had bound up their lot with the rising northern power. On the other side of the mountain chain the feeling of the population was unmistakably different. The Catholic Bohemians and Moravians were devotedly loyal to Austria, as Frederick found to his cost by the difficulty he experienced in obtaining supplies and information when he had to make war there.

Strategically the acquisition was of immense importance. Silesia, when held by Austria, has been compared to a glacis in front of the great mountain-rampart which protects Bohemia and Moravia on the north-east. As long as Austria possessed it it was hardly possible for a Prussian army to penetrate to Vienna, while the Austrians could at any time march without difficulty into the heart of the Prussian kingdom.

CHAPTER 5.

The Second Silesian War and the Peace of Aix-La-Chapelle

The two years following the Peace of Breslau were years of almost unbroken success for Maria Theresa. England espoused her cause with enthusiasm, and besides providing large subsidies sent an army into Germany, which defeated the French at Dettingen (June 27, 1743). George II. himself was present, and showed great bravery in the battle, the last in which an English sovereign has ever personally taken part. Before the end of the summer of 1743 Bohemia had been recovered, Bavaria conquered, and the tide of French invasion completely rolled back. In Italy the Austrians more than held their own against the Spaniards. Everyone was now ready for peace except Maria Theresa, who thirsted for revenge, and demanded compensation for her losses.

Intoxicated with success, she cherished all manner of ambitious ideas. Alsace and Lorraine were to be reconquered from France; Bavaria to be incorporated with Austria. The late imperial election was to be declared null and void, because the Bohemian vote had been excluded. This had been done, after full consideration, on the ground that a woman could not be elector, and that therefore it was impossible for Maria Theresa either to vote at the election or to transfer her vote to her husband. Her claim to set aside the election was simply monstrous; she talked as if the Empire were an hereditary possession of her house.

Frederick not unnaturally became anxious. He feared lest she might turn her victorious arms against himself, and he had sufficient reasons for believing that she still aimed at the reconquest of Silesia, the Treaty of Breslau notwithstanding.

It was, moreover, impossible for him to look on with indifference while the Emperor, to whose elevation he had largely contributed, was treated in the high-handed manner proposed by Maria Theresa. It was, in fact, this consideration, far more to check than apprehension on his own account, or influence m me desire of conquest, that induced him to Germany, renew the war. The first Silesian War was undertaken in order to conquer for Prussia a position among the great Powers of Europe. The motive of the second was to secure her influence in Germany.

With this object he sought to form a great union of German princes to uphold the dignity of the Emperor, and to resist the Austrian pretensions. The project failed because patriotism and national life were nearly dead in Germany. The union of Frankfort, besides Frederick himself and the Emperor, had only two members—the *Landgrave* of Hesse-Cassel and the Elector *Palatine*. It was hoped that more would join when Prussia was once in the field, but they never did, and the Emperor's death soon brought the union to an untimely end.

Germany failing him, Frederick turned again to France, and there his overtures were favourably received, (Treaty with France, June 5). Mortified with the ill-success of their arms, and stung by the contemptuous manner in which Maria Theresa rejected their proposals for peace, the French had resolved to prosecute the war with vigour in the spring of 1744. Strange as it may seem, they were still nominally at peace. Hitherto they had acted only as auxiliaries. Now, however, France came forward as a principal, and declared war against England (March 15) and Austria (April 27).

Frederick's plan of operations for the approaching campaign was well devised but not well carried out. He made a serious blunder himself, and the French were shamefully remiss in performing the part assigned to them. It was agreed that France should send two armies into the field, one to act offensively in the Netherlands, the other defensively on the Upper Rhine, where it was expected that Austria would make a great effort for the conquest of Alsace. Frederick was then to invade Bohemia. This was certain to cause the recall of the Austrian army from Alsace, which was to be pursued and harassed by the French on its retreat. Everything happened exactly as had been expected, except that when the Austrians retreated the French omitted to pursue them.

On the night of June 30, the Austrian army effected the passage of the Rhine by a masterly manoeuvre executed in the face of the enemy. They were commanded nominally by Prince Charles of Lorraine, but really by Count Traun, by far the most skilful of the Austrian Invasion of generals. When the news reached Frederick, he began to prepare for his invasion of Bohemia. He did not declare war against Austria, but announced, through his minister at Vienna, his intention of sending auxiliaries for the defence and support of the Emperor. The Prussians marched into Bohemia in three columns converging on Prague. Two passed through Saxony, the third came from Silesia. Frederick had the Emperor's permission to cross the Saxon territory, and he was careful to commit no acts of hostility during his passage, as he still hoped that Saxony might be brought over to his side. Of this, however, there was no chance. Saxony was already in alliance with Austria, and later in the year, after Frederick had met with some reverses, she openly joined the enemy and barred his retreat.

Early in September the three Prussian columns met at Prague, and after a week's siege the city surrendered, (September 16). Frederick then, in deference to the opinion of Marshal Belleisle, but against his own judgment, advanced into the south of Bohemia with the view of threatening Vienna. He thus exposed himself to the risk of being cut off from Prague. Yet even so he would probably have been able to maintain himself if the French had fulfilled their engagements. But while he was conquering the districts of the Upper Moldau, the Austrian army returned unimpaired from Alsace. The French had allowed it to cross the Rhine unmolested, and had not made the slightest attempt to harass its retreat. They were only too glad to get rid of it themselves.

In the ensuing operations Frederick was completely outmanoeuvred. Traun, without risking a battle, forced him back towards the Silesian frontier He had to choose between abandoning Prague and abandoning his communications with Silesia, and as the Saxons had cut off his retreat through the Electorate, there was really no choice in the matter. So he fell back on Silesia, abandoning Prague and his heavy artillery. The retreat was attended with considerable loss.

Frederick was much struck with the skill displayed by Traun, and says, in his *Histoire de mon Temps*, that he regarded this campaign as is school in the art of war and M. de Traun as his teacher.

The campaign may have been an excellent lesson in the art of war, but in other respects it was very disastrous to Frederick. He had drawn upon himself the whole power of Austria and had learnt how little the French were to be depended on. His prestige was dimmed by failure, and even in his own army doubts were entertained of his capacity. But, bad as his position already was, it became far worse when the unhappy Emperor died, worn out with disease and calamity, (January 20, 1745). This event put an end to the union of Frankfort. Frederick could no longer claim to be acting in defence of his oppressed sovereign; the ground was cut from under his feet. Nor was there any longer much hope of preventing the Imperial Crown from reverting to Austria. The new Elector of Bavaria was a mere boy. In this altered state of affairs he sought to make peace. But Maria Theresa would not let him off so easily. In order that she might use all her forces against him, she granted peace to Bavaria, (Peace of Füssen, April 20), and gave back to the young elector his hereditary dominions, on condition of his resigning all claim to hers, and promising to vote for her husband as Emperor.

While Frederick thus lost a friend in Bavaria, Saxony threw herself completely into the arms of his enemy, and united with Austria in a treaty which had for its object not the reconquest of Silesia merely, but the partition of Prussia and the reduction of the king to his ancient limits as *Margrave* of Brandenburg, (Treaty of Warsaw, May 18). Saxony was then much larger than it is now, but it was not only the number of troops it could send into the field that made its hostility dangerous. It was partly the geographical position of the country, which made it an excellent base for operations against Prussia, but still more the alliance that was known to subsist between the Elector (King Augustus III. of Poland) and the Russian Court. It was probable that a Prussian invasion of Saxony would be followed by a Russian invasion of Prussia.

Towards the end of May the Austrian and Saxon army, 75,000 strong, crossed the Giant Mountains and descended upon Silesia. The Austrians were again commanded by Prince Charles, but the wise head of Traun was no longer there to guide him. Confident of success, they marched along with colours flying and bands playing, hardly expecting that the Prussians would venture to meet them. Meanwhile Frederick, at the head of 70,000 men, calmly awaited their approach, encouraging as much as possible the notion that he was too dispirited for action, in order that he might lure them on into the heart of his country, and there deliver a great battle. The encounter took place at Hohenfriedberg, (June 4), and resulted in a complete victory for Prussia. The Austrians and Saxons lost 9000 killed and wounded, and 7000 prisoners, besides sixty-six cannons and seventy-three flags and standards. Four days after the battle they were back again in Bohemia.

Frederick followed, not with the intention of attacking them again, but in order to eat the country bare, so that it might afford no suste-

BATTLE OF HOHENFRIEDBERG, 1745

nance to the enemy during the winter. For his own part he was really anxious for peace. His resources were all but exhausted, while Austria was fed by a constant stream of English subsidies. As in the former war, England interposed with her good offices, but without effect; Maria Theresa was by no means disheartened by her defeat, and refused to hear of peace till she had tried the chances of battle once more.

On September 13 her husband was elected Emperor by seven votes out of nine, the dissentients being the King of Prussia and the Elector *Palatine*. This event raised the spirits of the Empress-Queen, as Maria Theresa was henceforth called, and opened a wider field for her ambition. She sent peremptory orders to Prince Charles to attack Frederick before he retired from Bohemia. A battle was accordingly fought at Sohr, (September 30), and again victory rested with the Prussians.

The season was now far advanced, and Frederick returned home, expecting that there would be no more fighting till after the winter. Such, however, was far from being the intention of his enemies. In the utmost secrecy a plan was concerted for the invasion of Brandenburg itself by three Austrian and Saxon armies acting simultaneously. It was, of course, impossible that preparations for such extensive operations could go on without exciting suspicion; but it was through the indiscretion of Count Brühl, the Prime Minister of Augustus, that Frederick first received certain intelligence of the designs against him.

He saw directly that he must no longer hesitate about attacking Saxony, even though he might thereby incur the hostility of Russia. He calculated that the Russians could not be ready for war in determines less than six months, and he hoped that, before that time had expired, he should be able to dictate peace from within the walls of Dresden.

After joining his Silesian army at Liegnitz, Frederick hastened northwards to intercept Prince Charles, who, at the head of 40,000 Austrians and Saxons, was advancing through Saxon Lusatia upon Frankfort-on-the-Oder. The king's movements were effected with such rapidity and secrecy that Prince Charles had no suspicion of his being in the neighbourhood. As he marched on in careless confidence, with his army extended in a long straggling line, Frederick suddenly fell on the Saxon troops who formed his vanguard, and inflicted on them a severe defeat at village of Hennersdorf, (November 23). Prince Charles had to fall back on Bohemia, while Frederick advanced into Lusatia as far as Bautzen. Some three weeks afterwards the Prince of Dessau defeated a second Saxon and Austrian army at Kesselsdorf, (December 15), a few miles from Dresden. This victory completed the subjugation of Saxony, and put an end to the war.

Three days after Kesselsdorf, Frederick entered Dresden, and astonished every one by the graciousness of his behaviour, and by the moderation of his terms. From Saxony he exacted no cession of territory, but merely a contribution of 1,000,000 *thalers* (150,000*l.*) towards the expenses of the war. From Austria he demanded a guarantee of the treaty of Breslau, in return for which he agreed to recognize Francis as Emperor. Peace was signed on Christmas Day, and the King of Prussia. returning home to the country which he had saved from imminent peril, was hailed by universal acclamation as Frederick the Great.

The Peace of Dresden restored tranquillity to the Empire, but the European war was protracted for nearly three years longer. The French won battles and took fortresses in the Netherlands, while the Austrians got the upper hand of their enemies in Italy. In the summer of 1745 Prince Charles Edward Stuart, son of the Pretender, landed in Scotland, and raised a rebellion which shook the throne of George II. to its foundation. The rebellion was, however, suppressed in the following year, and from that time forth the House of Hanover was freed from all danger from the partisans of the exiled family.

The war was at length brought to an end by the exhaustion of the belligerents. The peace of Aix-la-Chapelle, (October 1748), restored the state of affairs that had subsisted at the death of Charles VI. With only one exception of importance. That exception was Silesia, which in spite of the opposition of Austria, was formally guaranteed to Prussia. France gave up her conquests in the Netherlands, and received back Cape Breton in North America, which had been taken by the English. Parma, Piacenza, and Guastalla were erected into a principality in favour of Don Philip, the third son of the King of Spain, and certain cessions of territory that Austria had made to Sardinia were confirmed. The questions that had occasioned the war between England and Spain were quietly dropped.

Thus ended the war of the Austrian Succession, a war which for Austria and Prussia may be looked upon as the cause of the far greater and more bloody Seven Years' War. For England and France the two wars were really one, divided into two parts by an ill-observed truce of eight years.

Maria Theresa was anything but satisfied with the terms of the peace. Instead of rejoicing that she had saved so much of her father's inheritance, she harped on her losses, and, forgetful of the great services which the English had rendered her, reproached them with the cessions which, as she asserted, they had compelled her to make. During the latter part of the war, a feeling of ill-will had been springing up between the Empress-Queen and her allies, who complained of her supineness, and expected her to make greater efforts in return for their immense subsidies. This feeling was artfully stimulated by France, who, with her traditional diplomatic skill, contrived to sow dissensions between the allies by pretending to offer Austria better terms in secret than England was publicly proposing on her behalf. It was mere trickery on the part of France, but it served the desired purpose. Already Maria Theresa began to entertain a vague idea of abandoning her old connection with England and Holland, and of reconciling herself with her hereditary enemy, France.

To France and England, on the other hand, the peace was very welcome, to France because she was thoroughly exhausted, to England because she was weary of a war in which she had no real interest. Unfortunately, in their haste glad of to conclude peace, the two powers neglected to settle properly a question which was becoming one of great importance, and likely to embroil them in fresh hostilities. This question arose out of the relations of the English and French colonists in North America.

Chapter 6

England and France

§1. The North American Colonies.

At the beginning of the eighteenth century, the English colonists in North America were settled along the Atlantic seaboard between the thirty-first and forty-fourth parallels of north latitude. Some of them claimed by their charters a right to the whole continent westward as far as the Pacific, their boundaries to the north and south being accurately defined. But in reality they extended no further inland than the Alleghany Mountains.

The French settlers, insignificant in numbers compared with the English, were scattered over a vast tract of territory. They occupied the country north of the Great Lakes and of the St. Lawrence, extending to the south of that river over what is now New Brunswick and Nova Scotia, together with the adjacent islands. Besides this they had settlements in the upper valley of the Mississippi, and at its mouth the colony of Louisiana.

By the Peace of Utrecht, France had ceded to England the Hudson's Bay and Straits, Newfoundland and Acadia, or, as it is now called, Nova Scotia. Unfortunately the boundary of Acadia was not accurately defined. Its limits had always been very vague, and the French asserted that they included only the peninsula between the Bay of Fundy and the ocean. The question was still pending when the Austrian Succession War broke out, and it was left unsettled by the Peace of Aix-la-Chapelle, which merely stipulated that the boundaries of the two nations should be as they had been before the war. Commissioners were to be appointed to settle the matter, but before anything could be done hostilities broke out between the French and the English on the isthmus connecting the peninsula with the Continent.

Nor was this the only cause of hostility subsisting at the time of the peace. The whole frontier line was almost as vague as that of Acadia, and about this period the French set up a claim to the entire basins of the St. Lawrence and Mississippi, thus uniting their own colonies to Canada and Louisiana, and cooping up the English in the narrow strip of land between the Alleghanies and the ocean.

This was of course more than could be endured by the English, and, to resist the encroaching spirit of the French, a company was formed in Virginia for the purpose of colonizing the Ohio valley. In March, 1749, the Ohio Company, as it was called, received a grant of 500,000 acres from the crown. The French soon heard of the scheme, and La Gallisonière, the governor of Canada, promptly despatched 300 men to trace and occupy the valleys of the Ohio and St. Lawrence. Plates of lead were buried in various places with inscriptions signifying that from the farthest ridge whence water trickled toward the Ohio, the country belonged to France, and the lilies of the Bourbons were nailed to a forest tree in token of possession.

No active steps were taken by the Ohio Company till the beginning of 1754, when a party of thirty three men was sent to build a fort at the point where the Alleghany and Monongahela unite to form the Ohio. A reinforcement of 150 Virginian troops, under George Washington, was shortly afterwards despatched, but before its arrival the first party was driven back by the French, who appeared in great force, and themselves erected a fort on the same spot, and called it Fort Duquesne, after the then governor of Canada. On July 3, the French attacked and defeated Washington at a place Defeat of called Great Meadows. This skirmish, unimportant in itself, is memorable not only as being one of the main causes of the war which resulted in the expulsion of the French from North America, but also as the first appearance in history of George Washington.

The home government was at last roused into activity. Early in 1755 two regiments of the line sailed for America, under General Braddock. Braddock, personally brave but a harsh ignorant man and a strict disciplinarian, was altogether unsuited for the irregular warfare of America, and his expedition was badly planned and badly executed. His contemptuous treatment of the friendly Indians, whose warnings he neglected and whose assistance he despised, caused most of them to quit his banner in disgust. The result was that, when within ten miles of Fort Duquesne, the English blundered into an ambuscade and were defeated with terrible slaughter, Braddock himself being mortally wounded, (July 9). Farther north on the frontiers of Nova Scotia and New England the English were more successful, but their victories in this quarter were overshadowed by Braddock's disaster, and consternation prevailed through the colonies.

§2. NEWCASTLE AND PITT.

The government of England was at this juncture in the incompetent hands of Thomas Pelham, Duke of Newcastle, who after being Secretary of State for thirty years had become First Lord of the Treasury and Prime Minister upon the death of his brother Henry in March 1754. Newcastle had none of the qualities of a statesman; he owed his position to his immense wealth, his high connexions, and his great parliamentary influence, supplemented by a love of power seldom equalled in its intensity. He was a master of all the little arts by which it could be gained and preserved; there was nothing he would not stoop to in order to secure it, and his great skill in discerning the winning side, and in attaching himself to it, was hampered by no scruples. Sir Robert Walpole, his colleague for eighteen years, said of him, "his name is perfidy."

But it was only in the tenacity with which he pursued and clung to power that Newcastle showed strength or determination. In the actual exercise of it he was weak and vacillating, fussy and pretentious, jealous of everybody, and while peevish and irritable to his friends and dependents, timid and obsequious towards those whose influence or abilities he dreaded. Indefatigable in the transaction of business, he was, as Horace Walpole says, only always doing it, never did it. Always in a hurry but seldom punctual, he seemed, as one of his friends observed, to have lost half an hour in the morning, and to be continually pursuing without ever overtaking it. His quick shuffling gait, and the rapid stutter in which he poured forth his confused ideas, were the laughing-stock of his contemporaries.

Of his ignorance many anecdotes are told. Thus, when it was suggested to him that something ought to be done for the defence of Annapolis, "Annapolis," he replied, "Annapolis! oh! yes, Annapolis must be defended; to be sure, Annapolis should be defended—pray where is Annapolis?" The following is even more ludicrous. "Cape Breton an island, wonderful!—show it me in the map. So it is, sure enough. My dear sir, you always bring us good news. I must go and tell the king that Cape Breton is an island!"

Yet in his favour it must be said that in private life he bore a high character, and was generally regarded with affection; also that his ambition was pecuniarily disinterested. His life was spent in corrupting others, but he himself remained incorrupt, and after forty years of office he quitted public life considerably poorer than he entered it.

When Henry Pelham died, after a premiership of eleven years, George II. said, "Now I shall have no more peace," and the events of the next three years fully justified his fear. Pelham was no genius, but he managed the House of Commons with great adroitness, and by his conciliatory disposition induced men of the most divergent views to serve under him. During the latter part of his administration there had been no opposition whatever, because everyone who could possibly be dangerous to the Government was taken into it. There was little chance that the turbulent spirits who had yielded to the tact of Pelham would submit to the control of his feeble brother.

But the experiment had to be tried. Newcastle's position and parliamentary influence made him master of the situation, for he could have brought the Government to a standstill if he had been thrown into opposition. Though the recognised head of the Whig aristocracy, he had been content with a subordinate position during the lifetime of his brother, whose superior sense and ability he acknowledged; but even of him he had been bitterly jealous, and there was no one else to whom he would concede the patronage and influence of the Treasury. A leader of the Commons had then to be appointed, for this post also became vacant by Pelham's death, but it was doubtful whether Newcastle could bring himself to give up enough power to induce any first-rate man to accept it. There were three men in the House any one of whom might fairly aspire to it—Pitt, Fox, and Murray—and besides them none.

William Pitt, afterwards Earl of Chatham, was at this period in the forty-sixth year of his age. He was born in November, 1708, the second son of a gentleman of old and respectable family. He was educated at Eton and Oxford, but left the university without taking a degree, because of the gout, from which even at that early age he suffered severely. After spending some time in foreign travel, he obtained on his return home a cornetcy in the Blues, and in 1735 entered Parliament as member for the family borough of Old Sarum.

Walpole was then at the zenith of his power, though the forces which eventually overthrew him were gathering strength. The Tories, strong in the country, were insignificant in Parliament, but a formidable opposition to the great Whig minister was growing up within the ranks of his own followers, of whom many were discontented with his measures, or disgusted with his monopoly of power. Outside Parliament this party was supported by the favour of Frederick, Prince of Wales, who, after the manner of heirs-apparent in the House of Hanover, had quarrelled with his father, and was then raising the standard of opposition to the Court. Pitt threw in his lot with the discontented Whigs, and soon made himself conspicuous by the violence of his invectives. Walpole is reported to have said, "We must at all events muzzle this terrible cornet of horse," and he deprived him of his commission.

In the factious proceedings which led to the Spanish War and to the downfall of Walpole (1742), Pitt took a prominent part, but as he was not included in the new administration formed under the leadership of Lord Carteret, he remained in opposition till November, 1744, when the Pelham party in the cabinet obtained the mastery, and succeeded in driving Carteret from office. After securing the victory the Pelhams proceeded to form a government on what was called the "Broad Bottom" principle of selecting men from all parties alike. High office would then have been offered to Pitt but for the extreme dislike which George II. entertained for him on account of the vehemence with which he had declaimed against Hanover during Carteret's ministry. In the early part of the Austrian Succession War there was a very general feeling that the policy of the country was being made subservient to Hanoverian interests.

The feeling was in the main a just one, but Pitt, while constituting himself its mouthpiece, had allowed himself to make use of expressions unjustifiable in themselves, and most disrespectful to the king. He was, however, too formidable to be left in opposition by ministers like the Pelhams, so they pacified him with promises until, by the discreditable manoeuvre of resigning their places in the middle of the Stuart Rebellion, they forced the king to take him. Pitt wanted to be Secretary at War, but George stipulated that he should receive no office which would bring him into personal communication with himself, and he was made Vice-Treasurer of Ireland. Soon afterwards he was appointed to the of the lucrative post of Paymaster of the Forces.

This office gave Pitt an opportunity for displaying in a remarkable manner the disinterestedness of his character. It was customary for the paymaster to retain at his own disposal the floating balance, which was seldom less than 100,000*l*. The practice was considered dishonourable, and there was nothing underhand about it, for though it might occasionally cause great inconvenience, it was done openly by everyone who held the office. Pitt, however, poor though he was, placed the balance at the Bank of England, and refused to take a farthing beyond his regular salary. Nor would he consent to accept the commission of one-half *per cent*, which foreign princes who received subsidies from England were in the habit of remitting to the Paymaster of the Forces.

It was as an orator that Pitt first attracted the attention of the House of Commons, and, judging by the effect which his eloquence produced, as well as by the fragments which are all that remains of it now, he may without fear of exaggeration be pronounced the greatest ever heard within its walls. Many men have surpassed him in lucid exposition or in subtle and profound reasoning; many have been more brilliant in debate; but no one ever moved the House so deeply, or obtained so complete an ascendency over it. His sarcasm and invective were unrivalled, his bursts of eloquence magnificent, especially when he spoke without any premeditation on the spur of the moment.

On such occasions he was wont to be carried away by the torrent of his emotions to such an extent that he had to refrain from speaking when he was in possession of a secret that must not be disclosed. "I must not speak tonight," he once said, "for when once I am up everything that is in my mind comes out." Pitt's speeches owed a great deal to the personal advantages and rhetorical skill of the speaker. He was a tall handsome man, graceful in figure, and of a very noble and commanding aspect. When he spoke, his voice, at once majestic and melodious, riveted the attention of his hearers, and the fiery glance of his eye struck terror into the hearts of his opponents; he is known to have disconcerted a hostile speaker by a single look. He was a great master of all the artifices which could enhance the effect of a speech, and although his happiest hits were struck off in the heat of debate, his eloquence was in reality the fruit of long and elaborate training. The charge brought against him of introducing the manners of the stage into public life, is as deserved as the compliment from an unfriendly critic, that his acting was equal to Garrick's.

Oratory was the weapon with which Pitt gained and maintained his position in the House; but his greatness is built up on a more substantial foundation than parliamentary eloquence. Those who listened to his speeches felt that they were more than greatness. me re words, felt them to be the impassioned utterance of a man who would do great things if he could obtain the opportunity. The uprightness and vehement earnestness of his character, his pure and lofty patriotism, his nobleness of soul, his splendid imagination, and his power of animating others with his own enthusiasm —these were the source of his strength and greatness, and the marks that distinguished him from the herd of his contemporaries.

In an age of corruption, so degrading and universal that members of Parliament were not ashamed to take money for their votes, Pitt's stainless honesty stood out in sharp relief, and won him the confidence of the nation, which, though once or twice it wavered, never really deserted him as long as he lived. This public confidence was the basis of the "Great Commoner's" power, for he had no parliamentary interest, and he was far from being a royal favourite. Yet he was no seeker after popularity, and although his power rested on popular favour, he never shrank from risking it by setting himself in opposition to the popular will if he thought it wrong, no matter how strongly the current was running.

He was intensely ambitious; but if, like every politician of his day, he employed factious means to obtain office, it was for no mean or personal ends that he sought it. He sought it that he might raise the nation from the despondency in which it was sunk, and restore to it the spirit which it seemed to have lost. "I want," he said, "to call England out of that enervate state in which 20,000 men from France can shake her." And on another occasion, "My Lord," he said to the Duke of Devonshire, "I am sure I can save this country, and nobody else can."

With great virtues, Pitt had great faults. His career was marred by gross inconsistency, and, though this inconsistency was largely due to his earnestness and to the facility with which he was constantly carried away by the impulse of the moment, it is impossible to acquit him of subordinating his principles to ambition and resentment. Moreover, he was arrogant, self-confident, and of so overbearing a temper that it was very difficult for anyone to act with him. The ascendency which he maintained in his cabinet and in Parliament was not due to any tact in conciliating opposition, for of that he was wholly destitute, but simply to the fury with which he beat it down. What is more remarkable is that this proud haughty man was absurdly affected. As in public, so in private life and in the most ordinary affairs, he was always acting a part, always studying effects. Grotesquely theatrical and pompous even in the bosom of his family, he never allowed himself to descend from the lofty pedestal of his dignity.

Next to Pitt the foremost men in the House of Commons were Fox and Murray. Intellectually Henry Fox was fully the equal of Pitt. Without a spark of his impassioned eloquence, he was the best debater in the House, where he had attracted to himself a considerable personal following, and was looked upon by many as the natural leader of the old Walpolian party. Where he fell immeasurably below his great rival was in political morality. Pitt never had many parliamentary adherents, but his patriotism and integrity made him the idol of the nation. Fox, on the other hand, according to Chesterfield, "had not the least notion of, or regard for, the public good, but despised these cares as the objects of narrow minds or the pretences of interested ones."

William Murray, better known as Lord Mansfield, was Solicitor-General under Henry Pelham. His silvery eloquence and his clear, calm intelligence would have fitted him to be leader of the Commons; but he was not ambitious of the post, and he let it be understood that his hopes of advancement were purely professional.

Murray being thus out of the question, there remained Pitt and Fox. Pitt was at Bath ill with the gout, and, moreover, the king hated and Newcastle dreaded him. Newcastle accordingly applied to Fox, offering him the seals of Secretary of State and the leadership of the Commons. He, however, reserved to himself the disposal of the secret service money, and after a good deal of prevarication refused to disclose to Fox the manner in which it was employed. As this fund was used for the purpose of bribing members of Parliament, Fox very naturally observed that it was impossible to lead the House on such terms. "If I am kept in ignorance of this," he said, "how shall I be able to talk to members, when some may have received gratifications and others not?" In other matters, too, such as the filling up of ministerial boroughs, Fox found that the duke intended to keep all the power in his own hands. He therefore broke off the negotiation, and Newcastle, half glad to have escaped so powerful a colleague, at once conferred the seals and the leadership of the Commons on Sir Thomas. Robinson.

Robinson was a dull man, of moderate abilities and no parliamentary experience. He had spent most of his life as a diplomatist at German Courts, and was utterly unfit for the office with which he was entrusted. "The Duke might as well send his jackboot to lead us," Pitt exclaimed to Fox in contemptuous indignation. When Parliament met, the rivals, united by a common feeling of resentment, joined in attacking the unhappy secretary, and covered him with ridicule night after night. On one occasion, Pitt, aiming at Newcastle himself, bid the House beware lest it should "degenerate into a little assembly, serving no other purpose than to register the arbitrary edicts of *one* too powerful *subject*." He and Fox both held office under Newcastle, but the timidity of the minister prevented their receiving the dismissal they so richly deserved.

In January, 1755, Newcastle again opened negotiations with Fox. The terms offered were less favourable than those which he had already rejected. Fox was to have a seat in the cabinet, and to give a general support to Newcastle's measures, but he was not to be Secretary of State or leader of the Commons. Yet, to the surprise of his friends, and to the indignation of Pitt, who considered himself deserted, Fox accepted the offer. In the following November he was made Secretary of State. At the same time Pitt was dismissed from his paymastership in consequence of a violent attack upon the Government.

Of his speech only a fragment is preserved, in which he thus alluded to the coalition of Fox and Newcastle:

> I remember at Lyons to have been carried to see the conflux of the Rhone and Saone; this a gentle, feeble, languid stream, and though languid of no depth—the other a boisterous and impetuous torrent—but they meet at last; and long may they continue united to the comfort of each other, and to the glory, honour, and security of the nation.

His coalition with Fox propped up a while the tottering fabric of Newcastle's government, but events were approaching which required statesmen of a very different calibre.

§3. BREAKING OUT OF THE NAVAL WAR.

In the spring of 1755 it became evident that war with France could not be avoided. The nation was eager for it, but the king was hampered by fear for Hanover. The English navies might sweep the French from the seas, but the enemy would wreak his vengeance on the defenceless electorate. England was altogether unprepared for a continental war. There were positively only three regiments in the country, and Newcastle would not have any more raised from jealousy of the Duke of Cumberland, who, as Commander-in-Chief, would have the nomination of the colonels. The prospect abroad was equally cheerless. The foreign policy of George II. and of Newcastle since the Peace of Aix-la-Chapelle had consisted chiefly in subsidizing German electors to vote with Hanover in all affairs of the Empire, and to fight for her if required. But now, just at the time when they might have been of some use, the subsidiary treaties with Saxony and Bavaria were on the point of expiring, Austria, too, showed an inclination to desert her old ally.

On being asked what she would do for the defence of Hanover and the Netherlands should they be attacked by France, she made all sorts of difficulties, and threw the whole burden of the war on England, whom she recommended to contract subsidiary treaties with Russia, Saxony, Bavaria, Hesse, &c. It soon appeared what the meaning of it all was. Austria would support England cordially on one condition, namely, that she should join with her in attacking Prussia. Now, though George II. hated his nephew, and dreaded him almost as much as he dreaded France, he was not prepared to go so far as that; and even if he had been, he knew very well that the nation would never consent to such a war. As, however, Austria's determination on this point was final, negotiations were broken off, (June 1755), and thus ended an alliance on which for three-quarters of a century the balance of power had been supposed to rest.

Yet in this breakdown of the old system neither George nor his ministers were capable of devising a fresh one; they went mechanically on with the foreign measures that Austria had recommended. A treaty with Hesse had already been signed; another was being negotiated with Russia, in virtue of which the *Czarina* was to furnish 55,000 troops for the defence of Hanover, and receive in return 500, 000*l.* a year. The helpless hand-to-mouth character of the English foreign policy is conspicuously displayed by this Russian treaty. The rock on which the Austrian alliance had been wrecked was Prussia, and it was against this very Prussia that the *Czarina's* troops were destined to act. The treaty was signed on September 30, and the year was hardly out before it became worse than superfluous.

Frederick the Great heard of it and took the alarm. He had for some time been aware, as will presently be shown, that Austria, Russia, and perhaps Saxony, were leagued together for the purpose of partitioning his dominions on the first opportunity, and he foresaw the possibility of the English subsidy setting the combination in motion. He therefore determined to draw closer to England, so that he might either avert the threatened attack, or at any rate have Russia for him and not against him when war came. This was the less difficult since the English Court, with a curious inconsistency, had made tentative overtures to him during the summer at the very time when the Russian treaty was being negotiated.

As the two powers were equally desirous of keeping the war out of Germany, there was little difficulty in coming to terms. On January 16, 1756 a Convention of Neutrality was signed at Westminster, by which England and Prussia bound themselves to unite their forces to prevent all foreign troops from entering Germany during the expected war with France. The true interests of England were served by this measure, which brought her into union with the power that more than any other was marked out on both religious and political grounds as her natural ally. The connection was as yet slight, but the course of events soon drew it closer.

All through the winter, (1755-1756), England was harassed by fear of a French invasion; so great was the panic that Hessian and Hanoverian troops were brought over for the defence of the country. But the invasion never came; the ostentatious preparations made by the French all along their northern coasts were intended to cover a totally different design. On April 10, 1756, a large armament with 16,000 troops on board sailed from Toulon for the conquest of Minorca. Though the English ministers had received intimation of the preparation of this expedition months before, they persisted in regarding it as a mere feint, and did nothing to strengthen the garrison of Port Mahon, which was far too weak for the defence of the island. It was not till three days before the French fleet set sail that a squadron of ten ill-equipped ships was despatched to the Mediterranean under Admiral Byng. There is much justice in the bitter complaint of Horace Walpole, "this was the year of the worst administration that I have seen in England; for now Newcastle's incapacity was left to its full play."

The feebleness and indecision of the Prime Minister were reflected in his officers. When Byng arrived off Port Mahon, (May 19), the Castle of St. Philip was still holding out against a vastly superior besieging force. On May 20, a partial and indecisive engagement was fought by the two fleets, which were nearly equal in strength, The next morning the French were out of sight, but Byng, alleging their superiority in weight of metal and in men, sailed away and left Minorca to its fate. He seems to have despaired of relieving the island even before his arrival, and to have thought that any reinforcements which he might succeed in throwing into St. Philip's would only serve to swell the number of prisoners that would eventually fall into the hands of the French. Under these circumstances, he conceived it his duty to return and cover Gibraltar, which also was in a very defenceless state. There is no reason for charging Byng with cowardice, and on this count he was acquitted by the court-martial by which he was tried and condemned to death for neglect of duty; but he was certainly a weak, irresolute man, incapable of sound judgment and afraid of responsibility.

Left to its own resources, St. Philip's was, after a stubborn resistance, obliged to capitulate, and the best port in the Mediterranean passed into the keeping of France, (June 28). War had already been formally declared by England on May 17, by France on June 9. Another and greater war was on the eve of breaking out in the centre of Europe. Frederick of Prussia, satisfied that he was about to be attacked by a coalition, saw his only hope of safety in anticipating his foes, and towards the end of August he burst into Saxony at the head of 75,000 men. These two wars, separate at the outset, soon became blended in one, which is known in history by the name of the Seven Years' War.

CHAPTER 7

Policy of Austria During the Peace

§1. KAUNITZ.

The occasion of the Seven Years' War was the American quarrel of England and France; its cause was the determination of Maria Theresa to repossess herself of Silesia. But for this the traditional policy of Austria would doubtless have been maintained, and a great alliance might have been formed between England, Austria, and Prussia, which would have put an effectual curb on the power of France. For this, however, Maria Theresa cared comparatively nothing. As Mary of England said of Calais, so might she have said of Silesia, that the word was written on her heart. It is related that when she saw a native of the province she burst into tears. Its recovery was the cardinal point to which her whole policy after the Peace of Aix-la-Chapelle was directed.

Soon after the signing of the peace, Maria Theresa held a meeting of her secret council to discuss the future policy of Austria, the members of the council having previously been commanded to send in their opinions in writing. The general sense of the council was in favour of adhering to the traditional system of the monarchy, alliance with the sea-powers, England and Holland; and this course was warmly advocated by the Emperor, who thought it advisable to acquiesce finally in the loss of Silesia, and to seek to enter into more friendly relations with Prussia. Very different was the opinion of Kaunitz, the youngest member of the council, who, in a masterly paper, maintained that whereas Austria had hitherto had two great enemies to deal with, France and the Porte, she now had three, and that of these the King of Prussia was by far the most dangerous and irreconcilable; that Austria would never be safe until he was crushed, and therefore that the recovery of Silesia was an object never to be lost sight of.

At the same time, he added, it must not be attempted until Austria had formed an alliance so powerful that, humanly speaking, there would be no possibility of failure. Russia and Saxony would probably join with her, but that would not be enough, especially as Russian policy was too inconstant to be depended on. As it was hopeless to think of inducing England to concur in such an undertaking, he recommended that every effort should be made to obtain the alliance of France, which might perhaps be secured by cessions in Italy or in the Netherlands. The idea was not a new one, but Kaunitz was the first statesman who ventured to put it definitely forward as the guiding principle of Austria's foreign policy, and it was Kaunitz who ultimately succeeded in carrying it out.

Wenzel Anton, Count, and afterwards Prince, of Kaunitz Riethberg, was at the accession of Maria Theresa a young diplomatist in his thirtieth year. He soon attracted the attention of his sovereign by the clearness of his views and the lucidity of his statements, and, after being employed in various offices of importance, he was sent to Aix-la-Chapelle as plenipotentiary for Austria. On his return thence he obtained the complete confidence of Maria Theresa, and in the autumn of 1750 he went as Austrian ambassador to Paris, whence he was recalled two years afterwards to be placed at the head of affairs at Vienna. In April, 1753, he was appointed Chancellor of State, and for the next forty years he directed the foreign policy of Austria.

The character of Kaunitz presents a strange mixture of noble and petty qualities. He was haughty and supercilious, vain and ludicrously affected, foppish in dress, indolent and luxurious even to effeminacy. Yet the outward mask of a Sybarite concealed a remarkably keen-witted statesman, a man of marvellous discretion and great pertinacity, full of resources, and a master of his craft, subtle, wary, and deeply versed in the arts of dissimulation. A perfect if somewhat exaggerated type of the formal and pedantic, but refined, courteous and highly polished, diplomatists of the eighteenth century, his chief intellectual defects were his overweening conceit and vanity, which on one celebrated occasion, at any rate, betrayed him into an obtuseness contrasting strangely with his knowledge and powers.

The policy recommended by Kaunitz was cordially approved of by Maria Theresa, who was animated by intense hatred of Frederick the Great. Herself profoundly religious, she detested the heretical king for his well-known scepticism no less than for the wrong he had done her, and regarded it as a duty to bring back Silesia into the fold of the

Catholic Church. But much as Kaunitz wished it, it was not possible to put his views at once into execution. The political revolution he advocated could only be gradually effected; nor was Austria prepared for immediate War.

In the meantime searching reforms were instituted in every branch of the public service. The various provinces forming the Hapsburg monarchy were brought under a more uniform system of administration; the army was reorganized on the Prussian model, and the finances rearranged with such effect that Maria Theresa drew from her dominions a revenue considerably larger than her father had enjoyed when in the possession of Naples, Parma, Silesia, and Servia.

The first step towards the realization of Kaunitz's scheme was taken when he was sent to Paris, with instruction to seek to establish more friendly relations between the Courts of Vienna and Versailles, and to loosen the ties that bound France and Prussia together. In this he made very little direct progress. An enmity of more than two centuries' standing was not easy to remove, and Prussia was manifestly the best ally that France could have, though it might be urged with plausibility that the long rivalry of Bourbon and Hapsburg had served only to promote the aggrandizement of minor states like Savoy and Brandenburg, and that France and Austria united might dispose of the rest of Europe as they pleased. Indirectly, however, Kaunitz did a good deal. He saw the immense influence which Madame de Pompadour, the mistress of Louis XV., exercised over that indolent and enervated monarch, and he took great pains to gain her good will.

At no distant date the friendship of the favourite proved of great service to Austria (though not quite to the extent commonly supposed), but at that period Madame de Pompadour meddled very little in politics, and Kaunitz returned to Vienna dispirited and half inclined to abandon his project. Wavering between fear of losing England and hope of gaining France, he seems to have been really in great perplexity. There is little doubt that he would have preferred the English alliance to the French if he could have brought England round to his way of thinking about the Prussia; but of that he knew there was little chance, and before long he reverted to his original plan.

Thus it happened that, when England, in expectation of war with France, appealed to her old ally for assistance, Austria showed little disposition to afford it. The relations of the Courts of London and Vienna had been somewhat strained during the years that followed the peace of Aix-la-Chapelle, but harmony might easily have been restored if the interests of the two powers had been really identical, as they were in the days of the Grand Alliance, when both were equally concerned to resist the encroachments of Louis XIV. This, however, was no longer the case. England, as of old, wished to make use of Austria against France, while Austria wanted to employ all her forces against Prussia, who had been allied with France in the late war, and would probably be so still. Therefore as soon as it became certain that England would in no case join her in a war against Frederick, Austria ceased to strive for an alliance which no longer had any value for her.

§2. Negotiations with France.

Immediately upon the rupture of negotiations with England, Kaunitz renewed his efforts to obtain a French alliance. Count Stahremberg, the Austrian ambassador at Paris, was furnished with a sketch of the proposals that his Court had to make, and with a letter from the chancellor to Madame de Pompadour, couched in the most flattering terms, and requesting her intercession on behalf of Austria. It has frequently been asserted that Maria Theresa herself condescended to address the favourite in a letter, beginning with the words "*Ma cousine*," or even "*Madame ma très chère soeur*," but it is now tolerably certain that this story, though vouched for by contemporary authority, is utterly untrue. Nor indeed was such a letter in any way needed.

The *Pompadour* was easily induced to espouse the cause of Austria, not only for the sake of her friendship with Kaunitz, but also, and perhaps chiefly, out of spite against Frederick, who had mortally offended her by some satirical verses reflecting on her frailty, and by the contemptuous tone in which he habitually spoke of her. One of his sayings in particular had cut her to the quick. In the summer of 1750, when Voltaire was starting on a visit to Berlin, she had charged him with a polite message to the king, for whom she entertained a great admiration. Frederick, however, instead of receiving it in the manner anticipated, curtly replied, "I do not know her" ("*Je ne la connais pas*"). Voltaire at the time suppressed the ungracious reply, but three years afterwards, when he had left Berlin in disgrace, and with feelings of bitter disappointment and rage against Frederick, this and other delinquencies were faithfully reported.

Madame de Pompadour was therefore well disposed to further a scheme which would enable her to revenge herself on a prince who had treated her with contempt, and Louis XV. himself was inclined to look upon it favourably. He also had been wounded by the shafts of Frederick's wit, and he had, moreover, private reasons for desiring the Austrian alliance. Sunk though he was in the lowest depths of debauchery, he was preyed upon incessantly by religious terrors, and he believed that an alliance with Catholic Austria, formed for the purpose of warring against heretics, might atone for the evil deeds of a life of which he well knew the infamy, without having the resolution to amend it. This is no matter of conjecture; he actually told the Duke of Choiseul, that he believed that God would not damn him, if he, as king, upheld the Catholic religion, and that it was solely for the purpose of destroying Protestantism that he had allied himself with Austria.

On receipt of the Austrian proposals the King appointed to confer with Stahremberg the Abbé de Bernis, an early friend of Madame de Pompadour's, a man of considerable accomplishments but of no great abilities, and, except as ambassador at minor courts, without experience in the conduct of affairs. For some time communications were carried on without the knowledge of any of the Ministers of State, but there is no foundation for the common belief that the secret was withheld from them altogether, and that the treaty was concluded by Louis, the Pompadour, Bernis, and Stahremberg. Bernis was the principal agent throughout, and Madame de Pompadour had a great deal to say in the matter, but three at least of the four chief ministers were cognizant of the negotiations before any decided step was taken, and all were responsible for the result During the winter the Austrian proposals were frequently canvassed, but no great progress was made towards a definite agreement till the desire of the French Court for an accommodation was quickened by the conclusion of the Treaty of Westminster between England and Prussia.

Even in their altered state of things it proved impossible to draw France into active hostility against Frederick. The Treaty of Versailles, signed on May 1, 1756, was purely defensive; but Kaunitz was satisfied with having obtained so much, and regarded it as a stepping-stone to a closer union. Madame de Pompadour also expressed her delight at the settlement of an affair which she regarded as her own work, and assured Stahremberg that she would do her utmost to prevent an undertaking which had commenced so well from stopping half way. The expectation of Kaunitz was justified, and the promise of Madame de Pompadour redeemed, by the event. A year afterwards France was involved in a great alliance which had for its object the partition of Prussia.

§ 3. Austria and Russia

If France was as yet indisposed for an offensive alliance with Austria, this was far from being the case with Russia. For some time past the *Czarina* had been prepared to go all lengths with Maria Theresa. As far back as the year 1746, only six months after the Peace of Dresden, a treaty of alliance was signed at St. Petersburg by Austria and Russia, (June 2, 1746), which, though defensive in its general tenor, evidently contemplated a renewal of the war against Prussia. Seven years afterwards, a resolution was passed, (May 1753), at a meeting of the Russian Senate at Moscow, to the effect that it should henceforth be considered a fundamental maxim of the Russian Empire, not only to resist all further aggrandizement of the King of Prussia, but also to seize the first opportunity of overwhelming the House of Brandenburg by superior force.

The virulent animosity against Frederick which was felt at St. Petersburg rested on personal as well as on political grounds. The Czarina Elizabeth was a handsome, indolent voluptuary, grossly superstitious, and though by no means destitute of abilities, governed by the most unworthy favourites. Her life was only too open to satire, and Frederick unhappily was restrained by no motives of prudence in the exercise of his wit. His sharp sayings on Elizabeth and her favourites were reported by tale-bearers whose interest it was to sow dissensions between the two sovereigns, and the agents of the Austrian and Saxon Courts omitted nothing that could widen the breach. All sorts of stories, some true, some false, were told to the *Czarina*; she was even made to believe that Frederick sought to have her assassinated.

But it would be a mistake to suppose that Elizabeth was solely actuated by personal considerations. She was a daughter of Peter the Great, and ambitious of pursuing her father's policy of introducing Russia into the affairs of Europe as much as possible. She could not, therefore, look with indifference on the growth of a strong power on her western frontier, especially when its resources were wielded by a man so able and, as she thought, so unscrupulous as Frederick the Great. She had neither forgiven nor forgotten his invasion of Saxony in 1745, though the rapidity of the Prussian successes had prevented her interference.

Of Elizabeth's will to co-operate with Maria Theresa there could be no doubt after the Moscow resolution; the question was whether it was really in her power to render any material assistance. The sums of money which she squandered on her lovers were so immense that it was doubtful whether Russia could send any considerable army into the field. It was, therefore, necessary to procure an English subsidy for her if possible, and after repeated solicitations on the part of Austria, this object was attained by the Anglo-Russian Treaty of September 30, 1755. But the treaty was hardly signed before it lost its meaning by reason of the defensive alliance between England and Prussia.

The English Government, ignorant of almost everything on the Continent, was totally unaware of the *Czarina's* hatred of Frederick, and believed that, although the treaty was originally pointed against Prussia, it could use the Russian troops against the French in Hanover, or anywhere it pleased; indeed, it was by positive assurances to this effect that it had induced Frederick to sign the Convention of Westminster. It was, therefore, greatly confounded when Elizabeth absolutely refused to let her army act against any enemy but Prussia. The treaty was, of course, never put into execution; in fact, it was never ratified. But the mischief had been done already. Without waiting for the ratification, the *Czarina* had begun to assemble troops in Livonia, and she declined to be baulked of her revenge, merely because England had changed her mind.

In the spring of 1756, (April 12), Russia proposed to Austria a plan for the partition of the Prussian monarchy. Silesia and Glatz were to be reconquered for Austria, East Prussia to be conquered by Russia, and given up to Poland in exchange for Courland and other Polish territory on the Russian frontier. Hostilities were to begin in August, and as soon as they had commenced, Saxony and Sweden were to be invited to join the allies, Magdeburg being offered as a bait to the one, and Prussian Pomerania to the other. Austria, however, was not yet ready; she said that she must first make sure of France, and even after the conclusion of the Treaty of Versailles she gave the same answer. Negotiations for an offensive alliance were going on, and she had good hopes of gaining Louis by the promise of cessions in the Netherlands; but by the time all that was settled, it would be too late for military operations.

It was, however, definitely understood that hostilities should commence early in 1757. Such was the state of affairs when Frederick, aware of what was passing, determined to precipitate the crisis and attack his enemies while they were still unprepared.

CHAPTER 8

Commencement of
the Seven Years' War

§1. FREDERICK'S REASONS FOR WAR.

After concluding the Peace of Dresden, Frederick returned to Berlin in the full hope of enjoying, at least for some time, the tranquillity which his country greatly needed, after its efforts in the Silesian wars, (1746-56). He was, no doubt, sincere in his desire for peace, for he had much to lose, little to gain by a renewal of the war. For the next few years he was busy with law reform and other useful projects; but at the same time he went on continually strengthening his army, and laying up treasure year by year, for he knew well that, however peaceful his own intentions might be, Maria Theresa would never forgive the conqueror of Silesia.

It was during this period that "autumn manoeuvres" were introduced. Frederick devoted himself with great assiduity to the study of tactical problems, and then caused them to be worked out in practice by his troops. In 1753, 36,000 troops were collected at Spandau for this purpose, and the manoeuvres lasted twelve days. Prussian officers were brought from all parts of the kingdom to witness them, but great care was taken to prevent the presence of any unauthorized person. A cordon of sentries was drawn round the manoeuvring ground, and the chief magistrate of Spandau was even ordered to permit no one to ascend the church tower. After the Seven Years' War the manoeuvres were not shrouded in such mysterious secrecy, and foreign officers were permitted to be present at them.

It was not till 1753 that Frederick became actually aware of the designs that were being formed against him. Towards the end of the previous year his suspicions were aroused by information which reached him from Saxony, through the Prussian General Winterfeldt, whereupon he charged Maltzahn, his minister at Dresden, to investigate the matter by all possible means. Maltzahn succeeded in corrupting a Government clerk, named Menzel, who from Easter 1753 onwards furnished him with copies of various important papers in the Saxon archives, and of all the despatches that came from Vienna and St. Petersburg, together with Brühl's answers. Frederick thus became acquainted with the Menzel. Treaty of Warsaw, the Treaty of St Petersburg, and other documents, which convinced him that Austria and Russia harboured designs against him of a serious nature, and further, that Saxony, though she shrank from definitely committing herself, was nevertheless actively engaged in hounding Russia on. Additional information was derived from Maximilian Weingarten, a secretary in the Austrian embassy in Berlin, who was corrupted by Winterfeldt sometime in the year 1754.

It is manifest that it behooved Frederick, knowing what he did, to act with circumspection, so as to avoid giving Austria a pretext for attacking him. It was, therefore, with great apprehension that he perceived, in 1755, that the American quarrel of England and France was likely to be fought out in Europe, and that the French would seek to recoup their losses on the sea by attacking Hanover. This would bring the war to his own doors; his provinces on the Rhine and in Westphalia would probably become the seat of military occupations, and, worst of all, he himself would most likely be compelled to take part in it. His alliance with France was near expiring, and though it was purely defensive, the French would almost certainly insist on his joining their attack on Hanover as a condition of its renewal.

Indeed, it was not long before he received a hint to that effect. But this would give Austria the opportunity she wanted; if he attacked the electorate he would draw upon himself the whole power of Hanover, Austria, and Russia. Was he justified in running the risk? The conduct of the French in the late war showed how little reliance could be placed on them, and the hopeless imbecility into which the Government of Louis XV. had since sunk made them still less trustworthy allies for the future. Nor, indeed, did France seem to set much store by his alliance, or to pay much regard to his interests; while urging him to attack Hanover, she offered not the slightest guarantee against the probable consequences of such a measure. He began to suspect that France and Austria were secretly coming to an understanding, and therefore, as the best chance of preserving the peace of Europe, he concluded with England the Convention of Neutrality already mentioned.

Frederick's main object in concluding the convention was to prevent the invasion of his dominions by Russia, and he was careful to assure France that it was in no spirit of hostility to her that he had signed it, that he still hoped for a renewal of the defensive alliance, and that though he could not join her with against Hanover, there were many other services which he might be able to render. But his representations were without effect; probably Louis had already decided in favour of Austria. Anyhow, the Convention of Westminster was followed by the Treaty of Versailles.

The relations of the great powers to one another at this period was curiously complex. It was a time of transition from one system to another, and almost every one of them was in alliance with two others that were mutually hostile. Prussia had allied herself with England, but without abandoning her alliance with France. Similarly, Austria was in league with France, but had not yet definitely separated from England. Nor, again, had Russia, up to this time, broken with England, though she was meditating accession to the treaty of Versailles, and was urging Austria to an immediate declaration against Prussia, the King of England's ally. The course of events soon tore asunder the old ties, and ranged the powers afresh in two hostile camps. On the one side stood England and Prussia; on the other, France, Austria, and Russia, with several of the minor states.

The plot rapidly began to thicken. Frederick had not been immediately alarmed by the Treaty of Versailles; underrating the Power of Madame de Pompadour, and knowing that the best French statesmen still wished to renew the Prussian alliance, he believed that the connexion of France and Austria would be of short duration. He was, however, soon undeceived. In June, his ambassador at Paris informed him that the influence of the mistress grew daily, and that she and the king were meditating a closer alliance with Austria. At the same time he heard from Silesia that the Austrians were forming great camps in Bohemia and Moravia, while from various quarters there came news of the preparations of Russia. The *Czarina* made no secret of her intentions.

While deliberating on the best course to pursue under these alarming circumstances, Frederick received from St. Petersburg two anonymous letters purporting to come "in the strictest confidence from a very trustworthy source," which informed him that the threatened attack was deferred because the Russian army was not ready, but that it would certainly be made in the following spring. There is little doubt that the writer was the Grand-duke Peter, the acknowledged heir to the Russian throne, a devoted admirer of Frederick, and consequently a strong, though secret, opponent of the *Czarina's* policy. These letters turned the scale in favour of immediate war. Frederick saw his opportunity, and determined to draw the sword while he had only Austria to deal with.

It was a momentous decision, but it was just and wise. It was a just decision because, although apparently the aggressor, he was in reality acting in self-defence. There was no longer the faintest hope of preserving peace. The first Silesian war was voluntary on his part, but this time war was forced upon him. It was a wise decision, because his best chance of escaping destruction lay in anticipating the attack of his enemies. It was just possible that he might crush Austria in a single campaign, and nip the coalition in the bud. It is true that he was playing Austria's game by attacking her, for he thus enabled her to represent herself as the injured party, and so to call upon France for the succours stipulated for in the Treaty of Versailles. But he had reason to believe that delay would merely serve to give her time to draw France into an offensive alliance, and, therefore, this consideration was outweighed by the certain advantages of prompt action.

Still, in deference to the wishes of England, Frederick consented to make a final effort for peace before proceeding to extremities. Klinggräff, his ambassador at Vienna, was instructed to demand a private audience of the Empress-Queen, and to ask her whether her camps on the Silesian frontier were formed for the purpose of attacking Prussia. The answer was evasive. Klinggräff was ordered to press for a less oracular reply, and especially to ask Maria Theresa for a definite assurance that she would not attack Prussia that year or the next. Again the answer was evasive. Frederick had expected nothing else, and had made his preparations while awaiting it. It reached him on August 25, and four days afterwards he crossed the Saxon frontier.

Frederick had two reasons for invading Saxony, one military, the other political. His experience in the second Silesian war had shown him the danger of leaving the electorate hostile in his rear. In 1744, after he had passed through it into Bohemia, believing it to be friendly, it had risen against him, cut off his communications, and placed him in great peril. He was not going to commit the same mistake twice. In the second place, the originals of the Menzel documents were in the Dresden archives; if he could obtain and publish these, he would be able to prove to Europe that he was not the aggressor. It is sometimes maintained that while he had good ground for making war on Austria, he was not justified in attacking Saxony. This view is hardly tenable. Saxony, it is true, had not definitely committed herself by signing any treaties hostile to Prussia (at any rate since the partitioning treaty of Warsaw), but of the hostility of her intentions there was not the smallest doubt.

§2. THE INVASION OF SAXONY.

Frederick expected no resistance from the Saxon army, and thought that he would be able in a few days either to disarm it. or, as he hoped, to compel the King of Poland (Elector of Saxony) to yield it up to him and make common cause with Prussia. When this had been done and his route secured, he intended to pass into Bohemia and strike a blow at the Austrians in combination with Marshal Schwerin, who was to invade the country with a second army from Glatz. It was not improbable that a great victory might be won and Prague captured before the winter. The plan was well conceived, but it was foiled by an unexpected difficulty on the threshold.

The Saxon army, numbering no more than 17,000 men, was far too weak to resist the Prussians in the open field, but on the first news of their approach it retired, at the instigation of the French ambassador, into a camp of great natural strength. At Pirna, a few miles above Dresden, the low hills on each side of the Elbe rise into lofty and precipitous rocks intersected by chasms and covered with pine woods. Into this natural stronghold Augustus retreated with his army when he heard of Frederick's advance. The Saxons took up a position on the hills south of the Elbe, their right resting on Pirna, their left on the Königstein, an impregnable fortress built on a high rock overlooking the river.

As the position was too strong to be forced, Frederick was reduced to the necessity of blockading it. He was informed that the Saxons had provisions only for a fortnight, but, as it turned out, they were able, by means of short allowances, to eke them out for a much longer time. The King of Poland steadily refused to disband his army or to suffer it to take an oath of fidelity to the King of Prussia; he hoped that before he was starved out relief would come from Austria.

From the moment when war became inevitable, the Austrians had pushed on their preparations with vigour. In the last days of August, Marshal Browne began to assemble an army in the neighbourhood of Kollin, while Prince Piccolomini collected a second out of Moravia, and took post near Königgrätz, to resist an invasion of Bohemia from the side of Glatz. Their plan was to remain strictly on the defensive until the spring, to avoid pitched battles, and rather to suffer Frederick to occupy a portion of their territory than to run the risk of encountering him with inferior forces. They were therefore greatly disconcerted when they heard that Augustus had shut himself up at Pirna, instead of retreating on Bohemia, as had been arranged. They even suspected him of meditating an accommodation with Prussia, little guessing what a service he was really rendering them.

It was of course impossible to abandon the Saxons to their fate, and Browne was ordered to march to their relief with part of his army, and open out a line of retreat if it were still possible. This, however, was easier said than done. On the left bank of the Elbe the way was barred by the Prussians, and Browne's only chance was to work round by a circuitous route on the right bank of the river, to the rear of the Saxon position at Schandau. Closely blockaded as the Saxons were, messengers could pass to and from their camps by mountain paths, and Browne was able to inform them that he would reach Schandau on October 11. On the same day they were to effect the passage of the Elbe under cover of the guns of the Königstein, and on the following morning to attack the Prussian posts in front while the Austrians assailed their rear.

The intentions of the Austrians were not unperceived by Frederick. He therefore left one half of his army to blockade the Saxons, and advanced into Bohemia with the other. At Lobositz he fell in with Browne, and a well-contested but indecisive battle ensued, (October 1). The Austrians fought far better than they had ever fought in the Silesian wars. Both sides claimed the victory, but not with equal justice. The loss of the Prussians was greater than that of the enemy, but they drove the Austrians out of Lobositz, and kept possession of the battle-field. To them, therefore, the honour of the day must be ascribed, although the Austrians retreated in good order and unmolested, and, what was of more importance, Browne was able to carry out his plan of marching to the relief of the Saxons, just as if nothing had happened. His expedition was, however, a failure. From the first it had been little more than a forlorn hope; the ground was too difficult, and the Prussians too strongly posted, for the Saxons ever have had

Battle of Lobositz, October 1st, 1756

much chance of cutting their way through.

As a matter of fact, they hardly made the attempt. On the appointed day, Browne, with 8,000 picked men, reached Lichtenhayn, a few miles from Schandau, but the Saxons were not ready. Their pontoons had not been forthcoming at the proper time; the narrow mountain roads were choked by their artillery, and the Prussians harassed their retreat. They were two days late in getting across the Elbe, and then, wearied, half-starved, and drenched with rain, they were too dispirited to be led to the attack. Meanwhile, the Prussians had strengthened their posts on the north side of the river; Browne himself was in danger of being cut off, and had to retreat.

Nothing remained for the Saxons but to capitulate at discretion, Capitulation of Pirna, (October 16). The terms of the capitulation were severe. The officers were dismissed on giving their word not to serve against Prussia in the present war, but the rest of the troops were compelled to enlist in the Prussian army—a measure hardly justifiable and anything but successful, for most of them deserted on the first opportunity. Thus miserably for Saxony ended the first campaign of the Seven Years' War. But her sufferings had not been in vain. Fatal as it proved to her own interests, her stubborn resistance had saved Austria. By the time the capitulation was signed the season was too far advanced for military operations, and the Prussians were obliged to withdraw from Bohemia. Frederick had not come to Saxony as a conqueror, but from this time forth he treated the electorate as a conquered country. He took its government entirely into his own hands, and made it subservient to his own policy. Its finances were administered with Prussian economy, and during the whole of the war it afforded him a considerable revenue.

§3. THE WAR BECOMES GENERAL.

Frederick's first campaign was undoubtedly a failure. The possession of Saxony was very important from a military point of view, but he had not succeeded in making any impression on Austria, while the violence of his proceedings gave his enemies a handle which they were not slow to make use of. The papers found in the Dresden archives enabled him to publish a justification of his conduct, but this had no practical result. It produced a considerable impression in France, but upon the French Court it had no effect whatever. The king was completely fascinated by Austria, and the intrigues of Madame de Pompadour were now seconded by the prayers of the *Dauphiness*, the daughter of the King of Poland, who implored Louis to fly to the rescue of her parents.

All through the winter Austria strained every nerve to consolidate her alliances, and she did not scruple to use her position at the head of the Empire, in order to drag that body into the quarrel that had arisen between two of its members. On its own responsibility, without consulting the electors, princes, and cities, the Emperor passed sentence on Frederick, and condemned him, unheard, as a disturber of the peace. Many of the great cities altogether refused to publish the Emperor's decree, and even among the states generally subservient to Austria there were some that were alarmed at so flagrant a disregard of law and precedent. It may have seemed a sign of what was to be expected should Prussia be annihilated, and no state remain in Germany that dared to lift up its voice against Austria.

Nevertheless, in spite of this feeling, and in spite of the opposition of nearly all the Protestant states, Austria succeeded in inducing the Empire to espouse her cause. In all three colleges of electors, princes, and cities she obtained a majority, and at a diet, held on Jan. 17, 1757, it was resolved that an army of the Empire should be set on foot for the purpose of making war on Prussia. Some months later Frederick was put to the ban of the Empire. But the use of this antiquated weapon served rather to throw ridicule on those who employed it than to injure him against whom it was launched.

While all this was in progress the Court of Vienna was busily concerting measures with the Courts of St. Petersburg and Versailles. A new treaty was concluded with the former, (February 2, 1757), on the base of the Russian proposals of the preceding spring, and Austria bound herself to pay the *Cazarina* one million *roubles* (about 180,000*l.*) a year during the continuance of war.

Last of all, after long haggling on both sides, there was signed at Versailles a second treaty between France and Austria, a treaty for the partition of Prussia, Partition Treaty of Versailles, (May 1, 1757). Silesia and Glatz, and a certain small portion of Brandenburg, were to be conquered for Austria. Saxony was to get Magdeburg, Halle, and the adjacent districts, as well as the Duchy of Halberstadt, for which, however, she was to surrender part of Lusatia to Austria. The Prussian lands on the Rhine were to be given to the Elector Palatine, while Sweden, with whom France had already concluded an alliance, was to receive part of Pomerania. France and Austria reciprocally bound themselves not to make peace until these objects had been attained, and France undertook to pay Austria 12,000,000 florins (960,000*l.*) a year as long as the war lasted.

On the other hand, Austria promised that as soon as she had received her share of the spoil she would cede to France a portion of the Netherlands, including the seaport towns of Ostend and Nieuport, and give the remainder to Don Philip of Spain, Louis's son-in-law, in exchange for his duchies of Parma, Piacenza and Guastalla.

Such were the main articles of a treaty that was undoubtedly a great triumph for the diplomacy of Kaunitz and Stahremberg. Almost all the advantage was on the side of Austria. Not only were the territorial acquisitions which the treaty secured to her far more considerable than those which were to fall to the share of France, but the latter were contingent on the success of the whole undertaking. The loss of the Netherlands was no great matter for Austria; their remoteness and the conditions under which they were held made them rather a burden than a source of strength, and their fortifications had become so dilapidated as to be hardly defensible. And it was only a small portion of these Netherlands that France was to obtain; the greater part was assigned to a foreign prince, and it made little difference to France whether that prince were a Bourbon or a Hapsburg.

The indirect advantages of the treaty to Austria were greater still. If the war should be successful, the only German power that could offer any resistance to her would be annihilated, and she would able to extend her influence in Germany to almost any extent; nor would she any longer, as heretofore, be met by French intrigues at every turn. Yet it was for this that France was to spend her blood and treasure; for this that she was to neglect her war with England, to abandon her traditional policy, and to join with her hereditary enemy in destroying a power with which she had no cause of quarrel, and from which she had nothing to fear.

The adhesion of Sweden brought little material strength to the allies; but as Sweden was a Protestant power, it had some effect in discountenancing the rumour that Austria, France, and the Catholic part of the Empire were combining to put down Protestantism. The rumour had, nevertheless, some foundation in fact. Though nothing was said about it in the treaties, it is certain that both Maria Theresa and Louis looked upon their war against the heretical kings of England and Prussia as a religious war; it is little less certain that if it had succeeded, continental Protestantism would have existed only on sufferance.

It has been calculated that the population of the States arrayed against Frederick the Great amounted to 90,000,000, and that they put 430,000 men into the field in the year 1757. The population of Prussia was 4,5000,000, her army 200,000 strong; but, after deducting the garrisons of the fortresses, there remained little over 150,000 men available for service in the field. The odds against Frederick were great; but they were not absolutely overwhelming. His territories were scattered and difficult of defence, the extremities hardly defensible at all; but he occupied a central position from which he might, by rapidity of movement be able to take his assailants in detail, unless their plans were distinguished by a harmony unusual in the efforts of a coalition. His country was poor; but so far was it from being burdened with debt, that treasure to the amount of 2,750,000*l*. had been amassed during the peace.

If his troops were few in numbers compared with the hosts of the enemy, they were in quality inferior to none in Europe, and they were commanded by the first general of the age. Nor was it a slight advantage for Prussia that the commander-in-chief of her forces was at the same time the absolute ruler of the country, and able to dispose of its resources as he would. As such Frederick could run risks and endure defeats that no responsible general could have dared to incur, or have been able to surmount. Something, too, must be allowed for the enthusiasm likely to be called forth by the spectacle of a king leading his own armies to the battlefield, enduring the same hardships, exposed to the same dangers, as the meanest of his followers.

In addition to these resources, there was the English alliance; but for the first year of the war, at any rate, there seemed little chance of Frederick's obtaining much help from England. Later on, when Pitt was firmly established in power, she came nobly forward; but at the opening of the campaign of 1757, it looked as if England was likely to lean on Prussia rather than Prussia on England.

§4. ENGLISH AFFAIRS DURING THE WINTER 1756-57.

During the autumn of 1756 the English Government was too weak and distracted to be able to pay much heed to the great war on which it had embarked. The news of Byng's retreat from Port Mahon, and of the consequent loss of Minorca, raised a tempest of indignation throughout the country. Newcastle bent before the storm, and characteristically sought to divert resentment from himself by stimulating the popular fury against the unfortunate admiral. When a deputation of the city had made representations to him against Byng, he blurted out, "Oh! indeed he shall be tried immediately—he shall be hanged directly!" But it was of no avail. The unpopularity of his administration grew daily, and when Fox resigned the seals, weary at last of the position of a minister without influence, and of being, held responsible for measures about which he had not been consulted, no one could be found to take his place, and Newcastle reluctantly made up his mind to resign, (November 11, 1756).

Pitt's opportunity had at length arrived. A new administration was formed, of which the nominal head was the Duke of Devonshire, a nobleman of high character, but in no way remarkable for his and abilities. Pitt received the seals of Secretary of State, and Earl Temple, whose sister, Lady Hester Grenville, Pitt had recently married, was appointed First Lord of the Admiralty. Henry Legge became Chancellor of the Exchequer. It was felt from the first that the new ministry would be short-lived. Strong in talent and in the public confidence, it lacked two essential elements of permanence—royal favour and parliamentary influence. The King's aversion to Pitt continued, and Newcastle, out of office, retained great power in both Houses.

If, however, Pitt's tenure of office was insecure, he, at any rate, made his weight felt while it lasted, though disabled by the gout during the greater part of the winter. The King's speech, delivered at the opening of Parliament (December 2), was couched in a tone very different from what had been customary of late, and the actions of the ministry were in harmony with the policy it enunciated. 55,000 men were voted for the navy, 45,000 for the army; the Hanoverian troops were sent back to the Continent, and Pitt adopted the bold idea of raising two regiments from the Highland clans which had lately been engaged in rebellion against the Crown, a measure which more than anything else contributed to change the disaffection of the Highlanders into loyalty. A bill for the organization of a militia was passed through both Houses of Parliament, though opposed by the Lords, who impaired its efficiency by reducing the number of men to be raised to 32,340, one-half of what had been originally proposed. Reinforcements were despatched to America, and a daring and comprehensive plan was formed for the prosecution of the war in that quarter.

Nor was Pitt less determined to carry on the war on the Continent with vigour. Regardless of his former philippics against Hanover, he now loudly proclaimed the necessity of defending the electorate, and asserted that Hanover ought policy. to be as dear to Englishmen as Hampshire. He was equally resolved on cordial co-operation with Frederick the Great, whom he described, somewhat rhetorically, as standing "the unshaken bulwark of Europe against the most powerful and malignant confederacy that ever yet has threatened the independence of mankind." Unfortunately, Pitt's power was not equal to his will. His gout was a great obstacle to the transaction of business, and the king disliked him too strongly to be much influenced by his opinion in what he considered his own special department—the management of foreign affairs.

The measures for the defence of Hanover were concerted by the electoral ministers of George II., men without military knowledge, and animated by the traditional Hanoverian jealousy of Prussia. Frederick had suggested that an army should be assembled behind the River Lippe, using the strong Prussian fortress of Wesel as a place of arms, so as to cover both Westphalia and Hanover against a French invasion. His plan was, however, too extensive for the Hanoverians, who alleged against it that it would necessitate their entering the territories of the Elector of Cologne, who would then declare against them, and announced their intention of merely defending the Weser, thus abandoning Westphalia to the enemy.

It was in vain that Frederick urged that the Weser was not defensible, as it was fordable in several places, and its right bank, which would have to be maintained, was everywhere commanded by the left. When he found his arguments to be without effect, he ordered the fortifications of Wesel to be destroyed, its stores and artillery to be brought home, and its garrison of 4,500 men to join the Hanoverian army whenever it should be assembled.

The Hanoverian ministers were incapable of appreciating the military side of the question; but the chief cause of their want of enterprise was a negotiation which they were all the time carrying on with Austria, by which they hoped to secure the neutrality of the electorate by allowing the French troops to pass through it to attack Prussia. George II. never altogether approved of this perfidious scheme, but he allowed himself to dally with it till it was too late to do anything more than make a stand on the Weser. For this purpose an army was collected of about 50,000 men, including the contingents of some small German princes which were taken into the pay of Hanover, and of this force the Duke of Cumberland took the command soon after the middle of April, 1757. About three weeks previously a French army, over 100,000 strong, had crossed the frontiers of Germany.

The departure of the duke from England was the signal for important ministerial changes. The king had for some time wished to get rid of Pitt and Temple. Of the former he complained that he made him long speeches, which possibly Pitt and might be very fine, but were greatly beyond his comprehension, and that his letters were affected, formal and pedantic. As for Temple, he was so disagreeable a fellow that there was no bearing him. "I do not look upon myself as king," he said, "whilst I am in the hands of these scoundrels." The Duke of Cumberland, who had great influence with his father, and fully shared his dislike of Pitt, refused to quit England, leaving the king in the hands of a ministry he could not trust. Pitt's ill health was therefore made use of as a pretext for dismissing him, and the duke went forth with a light heart to a campaign which was to blast his own reputation and bring disgrace on his country.

Chapter 9

1757

§1. INVASION OF BOHEMIA.

The year 1757 was most brilliant of Frederick's life:—The later years of the war were perhaps more glorious, the years in which, with dwindling resources, he stood on the defensive against a host of enemies, keeping them at bay by consummate strategy. But the events of 1757 strike the imagination most forcibly; in no other year did the king gain such great victories, in no other did he experience so sharply the vicissitudes of fortune. The campaign opened for him with the brightest prospects. Entering Bohemia at the head of a vast army, he won a great battle which seemed to lay Austria prostrate at his feet, yet six weeks later he met with a disaster so crushing, as to appear the certain forerunner of his ruin. He was compelled to evacuate Bohemia, while his enemies, encouraged by the defeat of the hitherto resistless conqueror, closed in upon him from every side. Austrians, French, Russians. Swedes, and Imperialists, all fell upon him at once. His position seemed desperate, when suddenly rising like a lion from his lair, he scattered his foes by two great victories, each of which resulted in the total rout of the beaten army.

Unable to provide adequate means of defence at all points where attack was threatened, Frederick resolved to concentrate his forces against his principal antagonist, and to strike a severe blow at Austria as early in the year as possible. As soon as the snow was melted, and the roads had become practicable, an immense Prussian army poured into Bohemia through the passes of the Metal and Giant Mountains. As in 1744, it marched in three columns converging on Prague; two came from Saxony led by the king and the Duke of Brunswick-Bevern, the third from Silesia, under the command of Marshal Schwerin, who, at the advanced age of seventy-two, retained the vigour and energy of youth. The Austrians never divined Frederick's design until it was almost ripe for execution.

Affecting great trepidation, he had masked his real intentions, and lulled the suspicions of the enemy to rest, by putting Dresden in a state of defence, marking out camps in its vicinity, and erecting palisades and abattis on the roads from Bohemia. Concluding that he meant to content himself with maintaining Saxony, the Austrians on their side made preparations for an invasion of the electorate, later on in the year when their allies had taken the field. The news of the Prussian advance came on them like a thunderclap. Their troops, scattered through Bohemia, had to fall back on Prague in such haste that they were unable to carry off or destroy their magazines. In the first days of May, the bulk of their army was collected on the Ziscaberg, a hill to the east of the city. It was no longer commanded by the skilful and experienced Browne. The partiality of Maria Theresa for her brother-in-law had placed the incompetent Prince Charles at its head, and Browne, who was really a great commander, was subordinated to the court favourite.

Meanwhile the Prussian columns were rapidly closing in on Prague. Frederick had appointed May 4 as the day on which all were to assemble before the city; on the 6th, if the Austrians stood their ground, they were to be attacked and (such was his self-confidence!) beaten. Schwerin was a day behind the time, and, on uniting his column with a portion of the king's early on the morning of the 6th, begged that his soldiers might be allowed a day's rest, as they had been on foot since midnight, and had made forced marches for three days. Frederick, however, refused to be diverted from his intention of attacking that very day, influenced, there is little doubt, not only by the knowledge that a second Austrian army, under Count Leopold Daun, was hovering in the neighbourhood, and might at any time effect a junction with Prince Charles, but perhaps still more by an obstinate determination to carry out his programme to the letter.

The Austrian position was very strong. On the north, where Frederick and Schwerin were, the Ziscaberg was unassailed from its steepness. The eastern slope was much more gentle, but its brow was well defended by redoubts, and its base protected by marshy ground intersected by rivulets and by a string of fishponds, from which the water had been drawn off, and which from a distance looked like green pasturage, but were really a treacherous quagmire. Frederick determined, after reconnoitring, to attempt the Ziscaberg on this side, and brought his troops round accordingly. The Austrians, who were originally posted along the crest of the hill facing northwards, shifted their ground on perceiving his design, and wheeled their right wing round, until it was at right angles to the first position, so as to front the attack instead of being taken in flank, as would otherwise have happened.

The battle began at 10 a. m., (May 6), and for three hours raged with the utmost fury round Sterbohol, a farmstead on the lower slopes of the Ziscaberg. The Prussian infantry pressed impetuously forward, toiling through the marshy ground, and mowed down by the well-served Austrian artillery. Again and again they charged, and were as often repulsed, till Schwerin, maddened by the sight of his own regiment in retreat, snatched the colours from the ensign and rushed forward crying, "This way, my children." Almost immediately he fell, struck by five case-shot balls. The king himself brought up the second line, and, after strenuous efforts, Sterbohol was carried.

At the same time the Austrian centre was pierced by a bold attack of General Mannstein up the steep hillside, at the point where their right wing made an angle with the main body, while the cavalry on their extreme right was routed by Ziethen's *hussars*. Their ranks were thrown into utter confusion. Prince Charles, while endeavouring to rally his flying squadrons, was seized with a spasm of the heart, which rendered him unconscious; Browne had already been carried mortally wounded from the field. The battle was lost to the Austrians, and, though the fresh troops of the left wing still made a gallant resistance, they were gradually forced back into Prague.

It was not till eight o'clock that the fighting was all over on the bloodiest day that had been seen in Europe since Malplaquet. The Prussians had purchased their victory dearly, with the loss of at least 12,500 of their finest troops, besides old Schwerin, who, as Frederick said, alone was worth above 10,000. The Austrians lost 13,000, including prisoners. The numbers engaged on each side were about equal, the Austrians being 65,000, the Prussians 64,000. The victory might have been more complete but for an unlucky accident. A considerable portion of the Prussian army had been left on the west bank of the Moldau to guard the line of communications, and prevent an outbreak of the Prague garrison on that side. 15,000 of these, under Prince Maurice of Dessau, were to have crossed the Moldau, above Prague, in order to fall upon the Austrian rear, and intercept the fugitives; but Maurice's pontoon-bridge proved too short, and he was

THE BATTLE OF PRAGUE IN BOHEMIA, 6TH MAY, 1757

unable to get over the river.

Consequently the beaten army made good its retreat into the city, with the exception of 13,000, who escaped southwards, and eventually joined Daun. If Frederick had taken the advice of Schwerin, the miscarriage might probably have been avoided; he would not have had to fight with tired troops, and the nature of the ground would have been better understood; in short, the victory would probably have been more decisive.

The immediate result of the battle was the investment of Prague, where 46,000 Austrian troops were cooped up with little hope of escape unless relieved by Daun. Prague was not a strong fortress, but the presence of so large a force within its walls made a regular siege almost impossible, and compelled Frederick to have recourse to the slower mode of reduction by famine. The severe cannonade to which the city was subjected was ordered with the view of accelerating the process by destroying its magazines. All over Europe the blockade was watched with intense interest; events seemed to pause in expectation of the result, on which it was everywhere felt that the issue of the war depended. Frederick at first had little doubt that Prague would speedily fall, and intended as soon as it was captured to detach 30,000 troops to march through Germany, disperse the army of the Empire, and unite with the Hanoverians against the French. Then, after despatching reinforcements to East Prussia, he proposed to advance through Moravia, fight Daun, and, if all went well, put an end to the war before the year was over. Except Daun's army there was nothing between him and Vienna.

The actual course of events was very different. Week after week Prague held out, giving Daun time to march to its relief. On the day of the battle he was only twenty-five miles off, but on hearing of the Austrian defeat he fell back in the direction of Iglau, followed by Bevern, whom Frederick detached with 20,000 men to watch his movements. Every step that he took backwards brought him reinforcements, until at last he felt strong enough to recommence his advance. Bevern reported the altered state of affairs at headquarters, and the king hastened to his support with 12,000 or 14,000 men. More could not well have been spared from the blockade, nor did Frederick think that more were required. Unbroken success had inspired him with too great confidence in himself, and too great contempt for the enemy, till he thought that he could prevail against any odds.

On June 18 was fought the battle which wrecked the plans of Frederick the Great, and first taught him that he was not invincible. The Austrians, 54,000 strong, were drawn up in a well-chosen position on a low range of hills to the west of the little town of Kollin, and a mile or so south of the great Prague and Vienna high-road, along which the Prussians were advancing. Their left and centre were too strong to be attacked, but Frederick saw that an impression might be produced by throwing his whole force on their right wing. For this it was necessary for the Prussian army to pass in front of the Austrian lines, until it was opposite to their right, its march being not parallel to the enemy's position, but converging on it by means of a movement called the "oblique order," of which Frederick was very fond, and which he employed with signal success at Leuthen six months later.

The battle, (June 18), at first went entirely in favour of the Prussians. Ziethen's horse and seven infantry battalions under General Hülsen (which formed their advance guard when marching into position, their extreme left when in order of battle) attacked the Austrian right wing at Kreczor. After some hard fighting they repulsed the enemy, and carried two heights defended by batteries, when they found themselves confronted by fresh troops, which Daun had brought up by the rear from his left.

If at this time they had been properly supported the battle would have been won; it was said that four fresh battalions would have done the work. But no reinforcements were at hand. By some strange mistake, which, notwithstanding all that has been written about it, has never been explained, Prince Maurice, who commanded the Prussian left wing, had directed its attack upon the wrong point. Instead of marching up till he was opposite Kreczor, and then fronting to the right and commencing his attack, he halted and fronted some 1,000 paces too soon, and assailed the Austrians at a point where they never ought to have been assailed, and where he could be of no use to Hülsen.

Nor was this all. Frederick had given the most distinct orders that the right wing should not engage at all, but remain on the high road as a reserve to be called up in case of need. But when the need came it was not to be had; the impetuosity of General Mannstein, who commanded a brigade in it, had involved it in a general engagement with the Austrian left, and it could not be recalled. These two mistakes lost the day. Instead of the whole Prussian force being massed on the point where most impression could be made, it was broken up into detachments, attacking disjointedly all along the Austrian line.

Battle of Kollin

The Prussian soldiers fought splendidly, but they were overpowered by numbers, and by the well-sustained fire of the Austrian artillery. Several regiments were almost annihilated. Yet the unequal contest was long maintained; and one time the issue seemed so doubtful that Daun had actually given the order to retreat, when a brilliant episode turned the scale in his favour. In the Austrian army that day there were three Saxon cavalry regiments which had been in Poland at the time of Pima. The commander of one of these regiments, Lieutenant-Colonel Benkendorf, saw his opportunity, and, without waiting for orders, made a furious onslaught on the shattered Prussian battalions. The Saxons charged through their broken ranks, and, as they sabred them down, cried out, "This is for Striegau!" Striegau being the name they gave to the Battle of Hohenfriedberg.

Benkendorf's attack was followed up by the other Saxon, and by some Austrian, cavalry regiments, and the rout became general. Frederick strove in vain to stem the tide and rally the fugitives, until his *aide-de-camp* was obliged to remonstrate with him, and ask, "Does your Majesty mean to take the battery alone?" The king made no answer, but paused and surveyed the battery with his field-glass, then turned away, and, seeing that the battle was irretrievably lost, drew off the wreck of his army. The carnage had been frightful. Out of 32,000, the Prussians had nearly 14,000 killed, wounded, and prisoners, and the loss had fallen almost entirely on their matchless infantry. During the night they retired towards Nimburg, with little molestation from the Austrians, who also had suffered severely.

The next day, at evening, the king rejoined the blockading force before Prague. News of the disaster had preceded him, but his soldiers would hardly believe it till they saw him ride into the camp with downcast eyes, followed only by a page.

The loss of the battle carried with it the loss of the campaign. Frederick was obliged to raise the blockade of Prague immediately, and to retreat from Bohemia. The retreat was attended with fresh losses from desertion, and from the unskilful tactics of his brother, the Prince of Prussia, to whom the command of a corps was entrusted; and when the king got back to Saxony, shortly before the end of July, barely 70,000 remained under his banner out of 117,000 who had entered Bohemia three months before. The Austrians followed him and took up a stronger position at Zittau, just across their own frontier, resisting all his efforts to entice them into giving battle. A kind of deadlock ensued.

During the greater part of August, Frederick sat confronting the Austrians in the Lusatian hills, barring their way, though unable to dislodge them. But he had other enemies to attend to, and could not sit watching the Austrians forever, so on August 25th he resigned the command in Lusatia to Bevern, in order that he might march in person into Thuringia, where his presence was urgently needed to check the advance of the French and Imperialists.

§2. THE FRENCH IN NORTH GERMANY.

While the events just recorded were in progress the French were making themselves masters of nearly all North Germany west of the Elbe. Their principal army, 110,000 strong, took the field before the end of March, crossed the Rhine without hindrance, and occupied the Prussian territories in that quarter. The command was then assumed by Marshal D'Estrées, a soldier who had gained some reputation in the Austrian Succession War, but with small military capacity. Upon the arrival of D'Estrées magazines were formed, and the army began to advance towards Hanover, plundering and destroying the property of friend and foe alike. Its discipline was very slack; many of the officers owed their appointments merely to rank and court favour; the common soldiers were badly paid, and sought to supply the deficiency by pillage.

To resist the invasion the Duke of Cumberland had been placed at the head of 50,000 men, of whom the bulk were Hanoverians and Hessians, the remainder being made up by contingents from Brunswick, Saxe-Gotha, and Lippe Bückeburg, with the garrison of the now abandoned fortress of Wesel, which, however, was before long recalled by Frederick, in disgust at the pitiful strategy of the general. It was a mixed assemblage, but the troops were brave and well-trained, and under a skilful commander might have offered a successful resistance to the great but badly organized French army. Such, however, the Duke was far from being. At the approach of the enemy he fell back behind the Weser, abandoning Hesse without a blow; and when, after long delay caused by want of supplies, bad roads, and the irresolution of their general, the French at last reached that river, he made not the slightest attempt to dispute its passage.

D'Estrées, impelled by urgent despatches from home, had at length made up his mind to fight, and after crossing the Weser, attacked the allied army at Hastenbeck, (July 26). The battle resulted in a victory for D'Estrées, not a very decisive one in itself, for both armies quitted the field under the impression that they had been defeated; but the French reaped as much benefit from it as though it had been a complete success.

Cumberland lost his head, and instead of falling back slowly on Magdeburg, where he might have acted in combination with Frederick, he hurried off northwards through Minden and Verdun, and hardly paused till he had reached the fortress of Stade, near the mouth of the Elbe. Thus Hanover and Brunswick were abandoned to the invader, and the road was left open to the central Prussian dominions, while the English commander ran blindly into a *cul-de-sac*, whence he could only hope to escape by an ignominious capitulation. The French, however, contented themselves with detaching a small body of troops to follow his movements, and then settled down to the more congenial occupation of gathering in the fruits of their victory. D'Estrées was no longer in command. An order for his recall had arrived a few days after the battle, and with it his successor Marshal Richelieu, an old courtier who had displayed much courage and some skill when in command of the force which conquered Minorca, but wholly unfit to be placed at the head of a great army.

Bad as the discipline had been under D'Estrées, it was far worse under Richelieu. D'Estrées had at any rate done what he could to preserve it, but Richelieu set his soldiers an example in pillage. So notorious was his rapacity that when he returned to Paris and built a palace it was nicknamed by the Parisians the Pavilion of Hanover. After sating himself with plunder, the French general turned northward in pursuit of the allied army, and the Duke of Cumberland began to apprehend that he might be forced to surrender his whole force prisoners of war. Richelieu, on the other the allied hand, feared to drive him to desperation, and doubted whether he could undertake the siege of Stade so late in the year; above all he was anxious to secure peaceful winter quarters for his army. Both commanders were therefore willing to accept the mediation of the King of Denmark, by whose instrumentality a truce was concluded.

The convention of Kloster-Seven, signed on September 10, provided that the auxiliaries in Cumberland's army should be sent home, and that the Hanoverians should be allowed to winter in and around Stade. The convention was, to all intents and purposes, a capitulation, but Cumberland protested so strongly against the use of the latter word, that Richelieu gave in, without considering the possible consequences of his concession. The difference between a capitulation and a convention is that the one is a purely military act complete in itself, while the other needs to be ratified by the respective governments. Cumberland had no idea that his father was likely to disavow his act, but he shrank from the ignominy of signing a capitulation; Richelieu considered the matter to be of no great importance, as he expected that the convention would be merely a preliminary to a treaty for the neutrality of Hanover, about which negotiations had for some time been going on at Vienna.

The convention excited great indignation in England. George II. recalled his son, and treated him on his arrival with marked coldness. In France also it was viewed with disfavour. Certainly, more rigid conditions might have been imposed, but even as it was, North Germany was placed completely prostrate at Richelieu's feet. The convention left him at liberty either to proceed against the Prussian territories of Halberstadt and Magdeburg or to co-operate with Prince Soubise, who with a second French army was about to attempt the deliverance of Saxony in conjunction with the troops of the Empire. He did both, but ineffectually. Some of his troops occupied the Halberstadt country, but in a desultory manner, with an eye to pillage rather than to military operations. He also sent a reinforcement to Soubise, but that did not prevent Soubise from being beaten.

§3. ROSSBACH.

The army of the Empire was very slow in assembling, and if Frederick had conquered at Kollin, it would probably never have assembled at all. Public opinion in Germany was decidedly in favour of Prussia, and in the Protestant States, at any rate, there was a widespread conviction that the Franco-Austrian alliance would be destructive of the freedom of the Empire and of the Protestant religion. The troops of Würtemburg, who had been taken into French pay, mutinied, and declared that they would rather be shot than fight for France against Prussia. Nor was this feeling confined to the Protestant States. After the battle of Prague, some even of the great Catholic Princes, such as the Elector of Bavaria, and the Elector Palatine, showed a disposition to withdraw from their connexion with Austria, and to conclude treaties of neutrality with Frederick. But the King's defeat at Kollin restored Austria's influence, and this influence was still further strengthened when Soubise's army issued from Alsace, overawing disaffection.

From the end of June onwards, contingents from the various States kept coming in to the rendezvous at Fürth, where they were drilled into something like discipline. Most of them were short of their numbers, and in many cases half the men deserted on the way. An army of some sort was, however, collected, and early in August it set out from Fürth under the Prince of Hildburghausen, and marched to Erfurt,(August 29), where Soubise, with the French vanguard, had already arrived. The junction had not long been effected when the allied commanders received the alarming intelligence that the Prussian king was marching against them in person, and Soubise insisted on falling back to Eisenach to concentrate his army.

Their retreat into the hilly and impenetrable country about Eisenach was a serious inconvenience to Frederick, as it was of vital importance to him to get a battle from them as soon as possible, in order that he might return to defend Silesia against the Austrians. His situation was becoming almost hopeless. From every quarter the tide of invasion came rolling in on the Prussian dominions. In the northwest the French were in possession of the Prussian territories on the Rhine and in Westphalia; and now that they had beaten down the resistance of Hanover, they might be expected at any moment to turn their victorious arms against the central provinces of the monarchy.

Further south there were the combined French and Imperialist forces, against which Frederick was then marching. In Lusatia he had left the great Austrian army ready, as soon as his back was turned, to advance into Silesia, or even into Brandenburg itself. In the extreme east the province of East Prussia was overwhelmed by more than 100,000 Russians, who desolated the country, and committed atrocities too frightful for description. The circle of enemies was completed by Sweden, who, when roused into activity by the news of Kollin, began to ship troops over to Stralsund for an invasion of Prussian Pomerania.

Hemmed in by foes on every side, it seemed as if the fate of Prussia was sealed already. Yet, with nearly a continent in arms against him, Frederick's courage and composure never forsook him. Resolved not to survive the overthrow of his house, he always carried poison about his person to be used in the last extremity; but in the meanwhile, until that extremity should arrive, he went on without once relaxing his efforts, manfully struggling against ever-increasing difficulties. He never gave way to despair, and if death was constantly in his thoughts, he, at any rate, meant to die hard. His burden of cares was aggravated by the loss of his favourite general Winterfeldt, and by domestic troubles, by the death of a mother whom he dearly loved, and by the ill-concealed dissatisfaction with which his brothers viewed his policy; but, strangely enough, in the midst of it all, he was able to find relief and distraction in the composition of endless *stanzas* of indifferent French verses. At no time in his life was he more prolific than in the unhappy months that followed Kollin and preceded Rossbach.

After more than two months of anxious waiting, of marching to and fro, of sending out detachments this side and that, Frederick succeeded in bringing matters to an issue with the French and Imperialists. About the middle of October he had been obliged to hurry off homewards on hearing that the Austrians were making a dash at Berlin. The affair turned out to be merely a raid of 3,000 or 4,000 light troops, who no sooner heard that the king was marching against them than they departed within twenty-four hours of their arrival, with an instalment of the ransom they had demanded, amounting to 28,000*l*. In effect it proved useful to Frederick, as his retreat emboldened Soubise to come out from the Thuringian hills, and thus gave him the long-sought opportunity for a battle. The enemy had got as far as Leipzig, and were preparing to besiege it, when they heard that the king was coming back after them, whereupon they fell back behind the Saale, and awaited his approach. Frederick followed, and took up a position a couple of miles to the east of the combined army with his right wing resting on Bedra, his left on Rossbach.

The little village of Rossbach, so soon about to become a memorable name in German history, lies in a country rich in historical associations. A few miles to the eastward, just across the Saale, is Lützen, where Gustavus Adolphus fell in the hour of victory. Not much further off to the south is the fatal field of Jena, where, half a century after Rossbach, Frederick's work seemed all undone in a single day. Rossbach itself stands on an undulating plain, sloping gently down to the River Saale, which sweeps round it in a semicircle on the south and east at a few miles' distance from the village. On the south-west the plain is bounded by the Unstrut, which falls into the Saale at Naumburg, and is crossed by a bridge at Freiburg, a mile or two above the junction of the rivers. Immediately to the west of Rossbach there is a hollow, through which a small stream winds away northwards to join the Saale at Merseberg, and beyond the hollow, on rising ground which commanded a view of the Prussian position, was the camp of the French and Imperialists.

The two armies were very unequal in numbers. Frederick had only 22,000 men with him; the hostile army was nearly 50,000 strong.

Of these two-thirds were French, the remainder being made up of the troops of the Empire and of a few Austrian regiments. Soubise himself was not over-anxious to measure his strength with the great commander, but his officers were eager for battle and confident of success. Their only doubt was whether they could win any glory by destroying so small a force as Frederick's; their only fear lest he should retreat and escape them. They had never met him in the field, and they talked contemptuously of doing great honour to this Marquis of Brandenburg by condescending to make a kind of war with him.

Early in the morning of November 5 a great stir was observed in the French and Imperialist camp, and soon afterwards a single division, under the Count of St. Germain, advanced and occupied a height opposite to the Prussian position and began cannonading. By 11 o'clock the whole army was seen to be on the march southwards, apparently making for Freiburg and Unstrut bridge. Frederick believing it to be in full retreat, resolved to fall on its rear later on in the day. But it was not retreat that Soubise and Hildburghausen were meditating. What they really intended was to work round to the left, or even to the rear of the Prussian position, and then commence an attack in conjunction with St. Germain. A glance at the map opposite will show the danger of this manoeuvre, especially when practised against an enemy famed for the rapidity of his movements. The combined army had to move in a great circuit round the Prussian position, exposing itself to be taken in flank while attempting to outflank the enemy. This was, in fact, exactly what happened.

By half-past two Frederick knew what they were aiming at. They had passed through Schevenroda; the heads of their columns had reached Pettstädt and were turning to the left towards Lunstädt. The order to march was given, and in half an hour tents were struck and the whole Prussian army was in marching order. Seidlitz, with the cavalry, was off first, and hastened to gain a position in advance—that is, to the east—of the French columns. Frederick followed with the rest of his forces, leaving a detachment to watch St. Germain The movements of the Prussians were masked by two low hills, the Janusberg and Pölzenberg, so that the French could see that they were doing something, without being able to tell what it was. Fancying them to be in flight to Merseberg, and fearing lest the prey should escape when almost within their grasp, they rushed forward in disorderly haste. The cavalry advanced at a sharp trot, and though the infantry followed at the double, they were soon left several hundred paces behind.

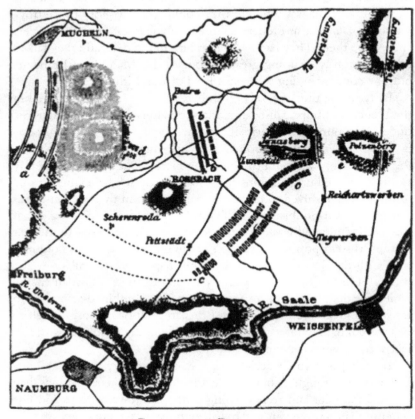

BATTLE OF ROSSBACH.

November 5, 1757.

a.a. Position of Combined Army.
b.b. Position of Prussian Army.
c.c. March of Combined Army to attack Prussians.
  d. St. Germain.
  e. Prussian Cavalry about to charge.
  f. Prussian battery of 22 guns.

At half-past three, (November 5), the French, Austrian, and Imperialist cavalry, 7,000 strong, were mounting the lower slopes of the Janusberg, when suddenly Seidlitz's *hussars* appeared over the crest of the Pölzenberg, and swept down on them, "compact as a wall and with an incredible velocity." The attack was utterly unexpected, and only four regiments were able to form in order of battle before the Prussians were upon them. In half an hour they were flying in wild disorder. By this time Frederick had got his guns into position, and from the top of the Janusberg twenty-two pieces of artillery opened fire upon the front of the French infantry, while seven battalions fell upon their right flank, marching straight up till they were within forty paces, and then delivering their fire. The French regiments, huddled together and unable to form properly, soon began to waver.

Then Seidlitz, who had reformed his squadrons at Reichartswerben, broke in upon them, and completed the confusion. At half-past four the battle was over. The Imperialist foot never came into action at all; they were swept away by the retreat of the French. Nor did the bulk of the Prussian infantry; the battle was over before they could get up. The French and Imperialists lost near 3,000 killed and wounded, besides 5,000 prisoners, and the greater part of their artillery and baggage; the loss would have been greater still if night coming on had not put an end to the pursuit. On the Prussian side there were 165 killed and 376 wounded. There was no sort of order in the enemy's retreat. No rallying-place had been appointed, presumably because defeat was a contingency that had never been contemplated. Very few regiments kept together, and the greater part of the army was scattered broadcast all over the country.

The effect of the Battle of Rossbach was marvellous. Not only in Prussia but in every German land there was great joy at the victory over the enemy of the whole German race. Never before had the French been defeated in a great battle by a purely German army, commanded by a leader of German blood. The rejoicings were intensified by the universal disgust which had been excited by the insolent and outrageous conduct of the French in countries to which they were supposed to have come as friends and deliverers. The army of Soubise was more disorderly and licentious than the army of Richelieu. Wherever it went there was the same tale of extortion, plunder, and violence; the doings of the French in Germany were compared with the doings of the *Cossacks* in East Prussia.

Even the fact that troops of the Empire had fought side by side with the soldiers of Soubise in no way diminished the general satisfaction of Frederick's victory. The German people were altogether opposed to the war with Prussia. Feeling that they were not adequately represented in the Diet, they were rather pleased than otherwise at the discomfiture of its army. If it helped to overthrow the old order of things in the Empire, so much the better. A new and better structure might arise in its place.

§4. SILESIA REGAINED.

Of the remoter consequences of his victory, Frederick thought very little, To him it was chiefly valuable because it set him at liberty to fight another battle in Silesia. It was high time for him to be back there. The Austrians had invaded the country in great force, and but for the timidity of Prince Charles and Daun, and their frequent disputes, Bevern must have fared even worse than he did. Eight days after Rossbach, Frederick started from Leipzig with 14,000 picked men, but though he made forced marches, a series of disasters occurred before he could arrive on the scene. First, the important fortress of Schweidnitz capitulated after a disgracefully short siege, with a garrison of 6,000 men, and stores of all kinds. Then Bevern was defeated in a great battle, which opened the gates of Breslau to the Austrians. Soon afterwards Liegnitz went too.

News of these losses kept reaching the king on his march, but nothing daunted he pushed on. resolved to stake all on a battle. Indeed, without a battle and a victory, everything was as good as lost already; the Austrians would take up winter quarters in Silesia, and the southern fortresses would certainly fall in the spring, even if want of provisions did not compel them to surrender sooner. "I will attack them," said Frederick, "even if they stood on the steeples of Breslau." The Austrians played completely into his hands. They had a strong intrenched camp before Breslau, and if they had stayed in it they could hardly have failed to repulse the Prussians, but they thought it a shame to sit still and be attacked by Frederick's little army, his Potsdam Guard-Parade, as they called it in derision, so they came out to meet him—and their ruin.

On November 28 Frederick reached Parchwitz, half-way between Glogau and Breslau, on the great road that runs through Silesia from end to end, where he was shortly afterwards joined by the remains of Bevern's army. Bevern himself was not with them; on the morning after his defeat, he had ridden out to reconnoitre, and had been made prisoner—intentionally, Frederick thought, but perhaps with injustice. After this junction the king had some 34,000 men under his command. The soldiers he had brought with him—the victors of Rossbach—were ready for anything, but the *morale* of Bevern's troops had been shaken, and until it was restored, there would be little use in leading them on what must have seemed, even to Frederick himself, almost a forlorn hope. He therefore assembled his generals and staff officers, and addressed them in a few well-chosen and stirring words. After recounting his recent misfortunes, he appealed to the courage, to the fidelity, and to the patriotism which they had so often manifested.

There is hardly one of you, (he continued), who has not distinguished himself by some honourable action, and I therefore flatter myself that, when the time comes, nothing will be wanting which the State has a right to expect from your valour. The hour is drawing near. I should think I had done nothing if I left the Austrians in possession of Silesia. Let me tell you, then, I intend, against all the rules of war, to attack the army of Prince Charles, though it is nearly three times our strength, wherever I find it. . . . I must venture this step or all is lost. We must beat the enemy or perish all of us before his batteries. . . . Remember that you are Prussians, and I am sure you will not act unworthily, but if there is any one among you who fears to run all risks with me, he can have his discharge today, and shall not suffer the least reproach from me.

The king paused, and seeing by the animated faces of his hearers the impression he had produced, continued:

I was convinced of it beforehand that none of you would desert me; I reckon, then, on your loyal help, and on certain victory. Now go into the camp and repeat to your regiments what you have just heard from me.

Then, changing his tone, he announced the penalties that would be inflicted on any regiment that failed to do its duty, and in conclusion, "Goodnight, gentlemen," he said, "soon we shall have beaten the enemy or we never see one another again."

Later on in the evening the king rode through the camp, and, as was his wont, spoke here and there a word of encouragement to the common soldiers. The enthusiasm of those who had listened to his speech spread like wild-fire through the whole army, and soon officers and privates alike were in a state of intense excitement, eager for the moment when they should be led against the foe. Patriotism and religion combined with the personal influence of Frederick to produce this result. Almost all the soldiers who were with him were native Prussians, the foreigners, of whom one-third of each regiment was usually composed, having for the most part deserted during the recent reverses.

So, when the king told them that without a victory all was lost, he struck a chord that would vibrate in all their hearts. They felt that they were fighting for their homes, and they felt that they were fighting for their religion, too. For though the war had never been avowed to be a war of religion, a very strong impression prevailed that such was really its character; and among the native Prussian soldiery there was a deep religious feeling, as was shown on the day of the battle when they advanced against the enemy singing hymns, and again after the glorious victory had been won, when a grenadier struck up Luther's grand hymn, beginning, "*Nun danket alle Gott*," and the strain was taken up by regiment after regiment, till, as daylight died away, its solemn tones were heard from every quarter of the battlefield.

The Parchwitz speech was delivered on the evening of December 3rd, and on the following day the Prussians advanced upon Neumarkt, where they surprised a party of engineers marking out a camp for the Austrian army on the hill beyond, and Frederick learnt, to his intense satisfaction, that Prince Charles was coming out from his entrenchments to meet him in the open plain. The next morning they were again on the march early, and at daybreak their advanced guard came upon a body of the enemy's cavalry just before reaching Borne, some seven or eight miles from Neumarkt. After this outpost had keen dispersed, Frederick rode up the Scheuberg, a hill close by, whence he saw the whole Austrian army extended before him.

The great Austrian army, over 80,000 strong, was drawn up in a line five or six miles in length, directly at right angles to the high road along which the Prussians were advancing. Its right wing rested on Nypern and was protected by bogs; its left extended beyond Sagschütz almost to the Schweidnitz Water, and was bent back at the extremity to avoid being outflanked. The bulk of the infantry was in the centre with cavalry on each flank, the right wing being commanded by Lucchesi, the left by Nadasty. In front of the first line were two villages, Frobelwitz and Leuthen, which were occupied by infantry and flanked by batteries, especially Frobelwitz, where the main attack was expected. It was not an ill-chosen position; it commanded the two roads to Breslau, and was not easily assailable on either flank; but it had one capital defect—its extreme length.

From his position on the Scheuberg Frederick could see the Austrians distinctly, though they were unable to get any clear view of him. The country about was a wide, undulating plain, affording. very few points whence an extensive prospect could be had, and the movements of the Prussians were in a great measure concealed by a low chain of hills, of which the Scheuberg was the highest. It was a great advantage to Frederick that he knew every inch of the ground; his Silesian reviews had made it familiar to him. An amusing story is told of how Daun, that morning, when out reconnoitring, asked a peasant the name of some distant object, and how the peasant replied, "That is the hill our king chases the Austrians over when he is reviewing here."

After a considerable time spent in surveying the Austrian lines, Frederick decided to mass his whole force on their left by means of his favourite movement, the "oblique order." Sheltered at first by the Scheuberg hills, the Prussian columns marched some distance southwards from Borne in a course parallel to the enemy's position. On reaching Lobetintz they formed in "oblique order," and so advanced diagonally against the Austrian line until they had arrived opposite to its extreme left. Having gained this position, they swiftly wheeled into battle order. The "oblique order" of attack was a manoeuvre invented by Frederick and frequently used by him. Its advantage consisted in enabling a general to mass his troops on a given point more rapidly than was possible by any other method, and outflank the enemy without running the risk of being outflanked himself; but it was a manoeuvre difficult to execute, and only to be practised with perfectly disciplined troops.

It may excite some surprise that the Austrians allowed Frederick to execute this manoeuvre under their eyes in broad daylight. The fact was that, since the loss of their outpost in Borne, they had been very much in the dark about his intentions, and what they did see only misled them. The movements of the Prussians about Borne and on the Scheuberg were visible, though indistinctly, to Lucchesi on their extreme right, and convinced him that the wing he commanded was about to be attacked. Upon this he demanded reinforcements urgently, and though Prince Charles and Daun for some time refused to accede to his request, they yielded at last when he declared that unless rein-

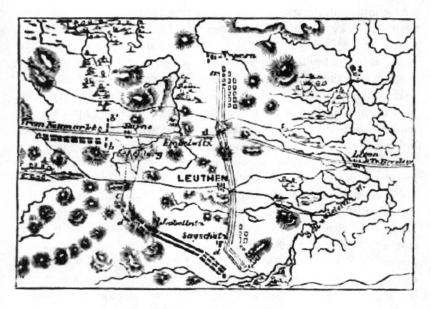

BATTLE OF LEUTHEN.

Dec. 5, 1757.

a. a.   Austrian Army.
b. b.   Austrian outpost at Borne.
c. c. c. Advance of Prussian Army.
d. d.   Prussian Army about to attack.

forced he would not answer for the consequences. Then Daun himself rode to the right with the reserves of the centre, and a large body of cavalry was ordered up from the left, which was thus weakened just when it ought to have been strengthened. Nadasty took a juster view of the situation. When the Prussians began to emerge from behind the hills, he saw clearly that it was he and not Lucchesi on whom the attack would fall. But it was in vain that he sent messenger after messenger imploring succour. Prince Charles was miles away in Frobelwitz, whence only a very imperfect view of the Prussian movements could be had. He and all the generals with him believed that the Prussians were retreating, so he turned a deaf ear to Nadasty's messages.

It was about one o'clock when the battle began. The Prussians advanced under cover of a well-sustained fire from their artillery, and especially from ten heavy guns taken from the walls of Glogau, and brought up with immense labour. Nadasty made a gallant but ineffectual resistance. The Prussians pushed on and captured a battery of fourteen pieces on a hill behind Sagschütz. When it was too late, Prince Charles saw the error he had made in massing troops on his right wing, and sent battalion upon battalion to the succour of his left. But from the distance they had to traverse before reaching the scene of action, they arrived breathless and in disorder, and were swept back with Nadasty's infantry upon Leuthen.

This village now became the key of the Austrian position, and the battle raged about it for an hour or so with great fury. By strenuous efforts Prince Charles had succeeded in wheeling his centre and right round into a fresh position, nearly at right angles to the first, and fronting the Prussian attack. The hottest of the fight was in Leuthen itself, where the church, the churchyard, and every enclosure was crammed with Austrian soldiers. The Prussian reserves were brought up, and the enemy were driven out of Leuthen; but still they stood their ground behind the village, crowded together in dense masses, and kept the Prussians at bay by the fire of their artillery. Then from their right Lucchesi came up with his cavalry to attack what seemed to him the unguarded left flank of the Prussians.

But the flank was not unguarded. In a hollow close by Frederick had stationed Driesen with the cavalry of the left wing, and Driesen, watching his opportunity, fell upon the Austrian horse just as they were going to charge. Lucchesi was killed, and his squadrons fled in confusion. The Austrian flank and rear were now exposed, and Driesen plunged into them and completed the ruin. A panic ensued. The Aus-

BATTLE OF LEUTHEN

trians flung away their arms, abandoned their guns, and thought only of saving themselves by flight When the twilight of the short December day came on, the battle was won.

As at Rossbach, the approach of night diminished the losses of the beaten army, but even as it was they were very great. The Austrians left 10,000 killed and wounded on the field, and lost besides 12,000 prisoners, 51 flags and standards, and 116 cannon. The Prussian killed and wounded amounted to 6,300. But the significance of the victory was not to be measured by the number of the slain. What was of importance was that the great Austrian army was so completely beaten that no thought of further resistance entered into the minds of its leaders. At noon on the morrow, Prince Charles commenced his retreat, after throwing rather unwisely a strong garrison into Breslau. The retreat was very disastrous. The weather was miserable, and the Austrians had lost their tents, and almost all their baggage. Thousands either deserted, or were taken by the Prussian cavalry, and when Prince Charles reached Bohemia, he had only 35,000 men under his command. Before the battle he had had, including the garrisons, close upon 90,000.

On the 21st Breslau capitulated, and its garrison of 17,000 men, with thirteen generals among them, became prisoners of war. A week afterwards Liegnitz surrendered, so that before the year was out Frederick was again in possession of all Silesia except Schweidnitz. This fortress was blockaded through the winter and taken by storm early in the spring.

A few words will suffice to dispose of the king's remaining enemies. After overrunning a large portion of East Prussia, the Russian commander Apraxin defeated in a pitched battle at Gross-Jägersdorf Marshal Lehwaldt, (August 30), to whom with 28,000 men the defence of the province had been entrusted. Apraxin might now have advanced to Königsberg and made himself master of the whole province: but instead of doing so he returned home, alleging that the country was too exhausted to support an army. Apraxin was influenced turns by political motives. The *Czarina* was dangerously ill, and if she should die, the policy of Russia would probably be reversed, as her heir was known to be opposed to the war. Even if she recovered, it was by no means certain that the Anglo-Prussian party in St. Petersburg would not get the upper hand.

As it turned out the *Czarina* recovered, dismissed Apraxin from his command, and ordered the army to recommence operations at once. This, however, was impossible, as Apraxin had brought it back in so wretched a state that months were required for its reorganization. Meanwhile the retreat of the Russians enabled Lehwaldt to march against the Swedes, who in September had invaded Prussian Pomerania with 22,000 men. Lehwaldt had little difficulty in dislodging them from the few places which they had taken, and in forcing them to seek refuge under the guns of Stralsund.

Never had Frederick's reputation stood higher than at the close of this memorable year: Leuthen alone, as Napoleon said, was enough to immortalize and to place him amongst the greatest generals. But his position and prospects were very different from what they had been after the Battle of Prague. Then he seemed on the point of forcing his enemies to submission. Rossbach and Leuthen had merely saved him from destruction.

§5. PITT AND THE WAR.

When we left Pitt at the commencement of the campaign, he had just been dismissed from office at the instance of the Duke of Cumberland. In less than three months he came back almost on his own terms. His dismissal spread consternation through the country. The stocks fell; the Common Council voted him the freedom of the City, and the chief towns of the kingdom followed the example of London by sending him their freedom in gold boxes. "For some weeks," says Horace Walpole, "it rained gold boxes." Various attempts were made to form a new ministry, but it was soon perceived that a government from which "The Great Commoner"' was excluded would have little prospect of stability. And Pitt himself had learnt something by experience. He had seen that great talents and popular support, though they might carry him into office, could not keep him there with the king and Parliament both against him. The king's favour could only be won by degrees, but parliamentary influence could be gained at once by a coalition with Newcastle. To this therefore Pitt consented. Newcastle also was ready to come to terms, having learnt that in a time of great public excitement the control of votes was insufficient to sustain a minister.

So the leader of the Whig aristocracy and the great representative of the people sank their mutual hatred and joined forces. They had little difficulty in marking out their respective provinces. Pitt, as Secretary of State, with Newcastle, a mere cipher, for his colleague, took the entire direction of the war and of foreign affairs. Newcastle, as First

Lord of the Treasury, had all the patronage of the Government in his hands, and was entrusted with the congenial occupation of corrupting members of Parliament. Their division of authority is well expressed by Walpole in a letter written the next year to a friend abroad. "Mr. Pitt does everything; the Duke of Newcastle gives everything. As long as they can agree in this partition they may do what they will." The king consented to the arrangement with reluctance, and complained bitterly of the perfidy of Newcastle, who seems to have promised him never to coalesce with Pitt; but opposition was useless, as the combination of Pitt and Newcastle was irresistible.

Several of the chief offices were given to friends or relations of Pitt, and Fox, who alone in the House dared to lift up his voice against him, was silenced with the Paymastership of the Forces. That Fox, after the prominent part he had taken, should consent to serve under his rival without even a seat in the cabinet, excited great surprise; but he was doubtless allured by the lucrativeness of the office, which afforded the means of repairing a fortune ruined by gambling and of providing for a family to whom he was devotedly attached.

By the time the ministry was formed, it was too late for Pitt to exert much influence on the war during the current year. The campaign in Hanover was hastening to its inglorious close, and ten weeks after Pitt took office, the Convention of Kloster-Seven yielded up the electorate to the enemy, together with the allied states of Hesse and Brunswick. French garrisons had already been admitted into Ostend and Nieuport as an earnest of their cession by Austria, a transfer pregnant with danger to English interests. Thus far England had met with nothing but disaster. In the Mediterranean, Minorca was lost, and the prestige of her navy dimmed. In America the war had been no less unfortunate; and to so low an ebb had public spirit sunk that an English admiral, cruising off Louisburg with seventeen ships, declined to engage the enemy because they had eighteen with a greater weight of metal.

Newcastle's pusillanimity seemed to be reflected everywhere, and so deep was the general despondency that Chesterfield, as calm and clear-sighted an observer as ever lived, could write:

> Whoever is in or whoever is out, I am sure we are undone... we are no longer a nation. I never yet saw so dreadful a prospect.

And yet, before Pitt had been a year in power, he had roused the country from its lethargy, and inspired it so completely with his own fiery spirit that the years of his administration may be reckoned among the most glorious in its annals.

Pitt's great triumphs were not due to any pre-eminent skill in the formation of his plans. In fact, from a military point of view, they were often faulty. The secret of his success lay in his all-pervading energy, in his skilful choice of commanders, and in his marvellous power of propagating his own enthusiasm an d inspiring with his own zeal all those who were entrusted with the execution of his designs. As was said long afterwards by one of his bitterest enemies:

> No man ever entered his closet who did not feel himself, if possible, braver at his return than when he went in.

His scheme of the war was judicious and definite. Avoiding the vicious system which in the war of the Austrian Succession had squandered the resources of England in seeking out France on continental battlefields of her own choosing, just where she was strongest, and where least permanent advantage could be obtained, Pitt concentrated his efforts on the destruction of her naval power, and the conquest of her colonies. Descents on the French coast were organized from time to time, with the object of destroying the enemy's arsenals and distracting his attention; but on the Continent itself, Pitt confined himself almost entirely to the secondary part of supporting Frederick the Great.

This support was given directly by means of a handsome subsidy, indirectly by re-establishing the Hanoverian army under an efficient leader, and so covering the king's right flank. Pitt's statesmanlike grasp of the situation convinced him that cordial co-operation with Prussia was the best way of saving Hanover; and that, even if Hanover were out of the question, it would be a fatal mistake for England to allow Frederick to be overwhelmed. He therefore induced George II. to break off the negotiations of his Hanoverian ministers for the neutrality of the electorate, to refuse his ratification to the Convention of Kloster-Seven, and to request Frederick to allow Duke Ferdinand of Brunswick to take command of his electoral army.

It may be imagined with what joy Frederick acceded to this proposition, which came to him a few days before Rossbach, bringing a ray of hope in the gloomiest period of his own affairs. No better selection could possibly have been made. Ferdinand was an excellent soldier, formed in the school of Frederick, whose service he had entered when a boy of nineteen, just before the first Silesian war. With great steadiness and decision of character he combined the tact and temper needed by the commander of an army made up of contingents from a variety of states, while his rank and position, as brother of the reigning Duke of Brunswick and a connection by marriage of the royal Houses of England and Prussia, gave him peculiar advantages for the difficult post.

In December the English Parliament met, and before the torrent of Pitt's eloquence all opposition died away.

Rossbach and Leuthen had materially strengthened his hand. The English had never wavered in their attachment to the Protestant hero, as they styled Frederick, with a just appreciation of his political attitude, and in complete ignorance of his religious sentiments, but they were naturally more disposed to go heartily into the war when they found their ally so capable of supporting himself. The Hanoverian army was taken into English pay, and a treaty of alliance, closer than that already subsisting, was concluded with Prussia, (April 1758), one item of which was the payment to Frederick of a subsidy of 670,000*l.* a year.

CHAPTER 10

Frederick Reduced to Extremities
1758–9

§1. THE LAST YEAR OF OFFENSIVE WARFARE.

The campaign of 1758, if less fertile in striking incidents than that of the previous year, brings into prominence the great strategical qualities on which, far more than on his battles, the military reputation of Frederick is based. Leuthen and Rossbach were masterpieces, but in his other battles there is usually something faulty. His marches and manoeuvres, on the other hand, always gave proof of consummate skill. The nicety with which his movements were calculated, the rapidity of their execution, and the organization which alone made such rapidity possible, are all above praise.

His plan was still, as of old, to strike swiftly at Austria before her allies could reach him. From the French he had little to fear now that the Hanoverian army was re-established under Ferdinand. The Russians threatened to be more troublesome. The *Czarina* had shown her earnestness and her disgust at Apraxin's barren campaign by sending Count Fermor in the depth of winter to take possession of East Prussia. Her armies might be expected in Brandenburg or Silesia as soon as the season was sufficiently advanced.

It was thought by many of the Prussian generals that the more prudent course would have been to remain on the defensive, but the bolder plan was more congenial to Frederick's nature, and preferable on political grounds as affording more hope of an early peace. So as soon as Schweidnitz was recaptured, he plunged into Moravia, and laid siege to the important fortress of Olmütz. The siege was not a success; Frederick's sieges were seldom well managed, and this one presented peculiar difficulties, Olmütz was a strong place, well provisioned and garrisoned, held by a resolute and experienced commander. It was not easy to invest except by a large army, because the Morawa flowing to the east of it was provided with sluices, by means of which the surrounding country could be laid under water. Above all it was situated at an immense distance from the Prussian base of operations. All supplies and munitions of war had to be brought up from Neisse, ninety miles off, and the greater part of the road lay through a rough and hilly country, infested by the light troops of the enemy, and inhabited by a population whose devotion to Austria made it very difficult for the Prussians to procure intelligence.

Under these conditions the siege commenced about the middle of May. Daun with a large army hung on the skirts of the investing army, and, while carefully avoiding a battle, impeded the operations of the besiegers, and threw supplies and reinforcements into Olmütz. Time and ammunition were wasted at its commencement by a mistake of the chief engineer, who opened his trenches at too great a distance from the fortress. At length, however, after lasting seven weeks, it was approaching completion, when it was suddenly brought to an end by the loss of a great convoy of 3,000 or 4,000 wagons.

The officer who destroyed the convoy was Major-General Laudon. Laudon had as yet held only subordinate commands, but he was by far the most capable general in the Austrian army, and soon eclipsed the fame of the prudent, timid Daun, the Fabius Cunctator of Austria, as they called him at Vienna. With the exception of Eugene he was the greatest general the Austrians ever had. In rapidity, energy, and inventiveness he was hardly inferior to Frederick, and if he had had the same control over the armies and resources of Austria that Frederick had over those of Prussia, the Seven Years' War might not improbably have ended differently. Like Eugene, and like many of the great Austrian soldiers, Laudon was a foreigner. He came of an old Scotch family which had settled in Livonia in the fourteenth century, and in 1731, when in his fifteenth year, he entered the Russian army and learned the art of war under the celebrated Marshal Münnich. In 1742 he quitted the Russian service, and in the following year offered his sword to Frederick of Prussia.

Skilful as Frederick usually was in reading character, he failed to discover any merit in Laudon, and contemptuously refused his application for a captaincy, saying, "the physiognomy of that man is offensive to me." Laudon then repaired to Vienna, obtained a commission from Maria Theresa, and eventually became the most formidable enemy Frederick ever had. In this respect, again, his fortunes present a parallel with those of Eugene, who was refused first a prebend, then a troop of dragoons, by Louis XIV., before he entered the service of Louis' great enemy.

The loss of the convoy compelled Frederick to raise the siege of Olmütz, and placed him in considerable peril. Want of supplies prevented his remaining where he was, and 25,000 Austrians were between him and Silesia, while Daun lay ready to fall on his rear as soon as he began to retreat. With great intrepidity he abandoned all idea of getting straight back to Silesia, and concealing his movements with much adroitness, turned his retreat into an advance, and marched into Bohemia, where he maintained himself until the news of a Russian advance into Brandenburg forced him to evacuate the country. He then recrossed the mountains, and with 14,000 picked men set out for Frankfort on the Oder. Arriving at Frankfort after ten days of rapid marching, he united his forces with the corps of Count Dohna, and prepared for battle. Fermor, hearing of his advent, drew up his army in battle order at the neighbouring village of Zorndorf. He had rather more than 50,000 regular troops, besides a large body of *Cossack* and Calmuck irregular cavalry. The Prussians were about 32,000 strong.

The Battle of Zorndorf, (August 25), was the bloodiest in all the war. It lasted ten hours, and was contested on both sides with savage fury. The Russians had been guilty of great and inexcusable barbarities n their march through Brandenburg, and the Prussian soldiers, many of whom were Brandenburg men, were maddened by the tales of cruelty that were told them, and by the sight of smouldering villages all around; the king himself, usually so calm and passionless, was exasperated into issuing the ruthless order that no quarter was to be given.

The Russians were badly handled, but they fought with dogged courage, suffering themselves to be shot and sabred down in their ranks sooner than give way, and the day would probably have been theirs but for the splendid behaviour of the Prussian cavalry, led by the brilliant and dashing Seidlitz. Late in the afternoon, when ammunition was getting scarce, the battle resolved itself into a hand-to-hand struggle, in which the hostile soldiery attacked each other with sabres, with bayonets, and with the butt ends of their muskets. Men wounded to death employed their last moments in butchering one another, and in one instance a Russian, himself mortally wounded, was found lying on the prostrate body of a Prussian gnawing it with his teeth. When

Battle of Zorndorf, August 25, 1758

the approach of night and the exhaustion of the combatants put an end to the slaughter, the Prussians had won, but Frederick had purchased the victory with the blood of 11,500 of his bravest followers; of the Russians, 21,000 had fallen.

Zorndorf, though not a very complete victory in itself, proved decisive of the Russian campaign of that year. During the night of the 25th the Russians maintained a portion of the field, but after hovering in the neighbourhood for some days Fermor found it necessary to retreat into Poland.

As soon as they were fairly off, Frederick was again on the march, hurrying towards Saxony to the relief of his brother Henry. Daun had taken advantage of his absence to invade the electorate in conjunction with the army of the Empire, which was now commanded by the Duke of Zweibrücken. Prince Henry, with some 30,000 men, was threatened by two armies, which were collectively nearly four times his strength, and though he occupied an exceedingly well-chosen position, it is obvious that Daun and Zweibrücken, if they had acted with vigour, might have crushed him before his brother could come to the rescue. Great expectations were cherished in Vienna of what was to be done during Frederick's absence. Rapidity, however, was not Daun's *forte*, and before he had attempted anything against the prince the king returned, having traversed 120 miles in seven days, a rate of speed that in those days was considered extraordinary.

His return reduced Daun to the defensive and was followed by a month of intricate manoeuvring in the Saxon hill-country, the king trying all he could to draw the Austrian commander into giving battle, the latter as steadily refusing it. At last Frederick gave his wary enemy a chance. While trying to manoeuvre him into fighting or retreating, he recklessly encamped in a position completely commanded by the Austrian army of twice his strength. He was aware of the insecurity of his encampment at Hochkirch, and intended to move as soon as he had received a convoy of provisions, but did not think the danger great enough to justify a retreat in the face of the enemy; in fact, he entertained an unmerited contempt for his antagonist, and thought he might take liberties with him. To Marshal Keith, who said, in remonstrance, "If the Austrians leave us unmolested in this camp, they deserve to be hanged," he coolly replied, "It is to be hoped they are more afraid of us than of the gallows."

The Austrians were of Keith's opinion. Daun saw his opportunity, and, while making ostentatious preparations for defence, secretly matured an elaborate plan for a night attack on the Prussian camp. When the church clock of Hochkirch struck five on the morning of October 14, the unsuspecting Prussians were roused from their slumbers by the fire of Austrian musketry. Almost any other army would have been ruined, but the discipline of the troops and the presence of mind of the king and his officers saved them from destruction.

Notwithstanding the surprise and the darkness, they flew to arms, swiftly but without panic, and made so stubborn a resistance, that after a terrific struggle of five hours they retired in good order from the field, beaten but not routed. The calmness and precision with which Frederick conducted the retreat excited the admiration of his opponents. The Prussians, had, however, suffered severely. Their killed, wounded, and prisoners amounted to nearly 9,000, and they had lost besides, 101 guns, 30 flags and standards. Among the slain was Marshal Keith, an excellent officer, and one of the few real personal friends that Frederick had. Francis of Brunswick also perished, and Maurice of Dessau fell, severely wounded, into the hands of the enemy. The king himself was slightly wounded, and had a narrow escape of being made prisoner.

On the same day died Wilhelmina, *Margravine* of Baireuth, Frederick's favourite sister, the companion of his childhood, the sympathetic friend of his youth, and his fellow-sufferer under paternal tyranny.

Daun's victory gave occasion to a ludicrous proceeding on the part of the Pope, who thought fit to present the Austrian commander with a consecrated hat and sword, in recognition of his triumph over the heretical Prussians, and in imitation of his predecessors, who had bestowed similar rewards on the champions of Christendom against the heathen. The stroke was not a happy one, for the age of Crusades was past, and the Prussians, though heretical, were not heathen. The papal gifts excited the laughter of Europe instead of its reverence, and betrayed the religious character of the war, which was just what Frederick always liked to insist on

The results of Hochkirch were not a little surprising. The Austrians had won a great victory but the Prussians reaped the fruits of it. After the battle Daun returned to his old camp, sang a "*Te Deum*" for the victory, and then entrenched himself as carefully as if he had been beaten, considering that he did enough if he barred the great highway to Silesia. Frederick, after retiring two miles from the field, called up reinforcements from Dresden, reorganized his army, and prepared for a fresh undertaking, just as if he had been the victor. "Daun has let us out of check," he said; "the game is not lost. We will rest here for a few days, then go to Silesia and deliver Neisse." Daun had no idea of following up an advantage, and Frederick was always greatest when he had to extricate himself from an awkward situation.

The situation was indeed awkward. Neisse and Cosel were invested by a second Austrian army, under General Harsch, and unless they were soon relieved they would fall, and all Upper Silesia with them, into the hands of the enemy. But between the king and his fortresses was Daun's victorious army, and even if this were evaded, his departure would leave Saxony dangerously exposed. So impossible did it seem for him to march into Silesia that Daun sent word to Harsch that he might go on quietly with his sieges since he could answer for the king. The apparently impossible, however, happened. Frederick managed to circumvent Daun's great army, set off for Silesia by forced marches, relieved Neisse, and returned in time to save Saxony.

The close of this campaign marks a definite stage in the history of the war. To all outward appearance Frederick's prospects were still fair enough. If East Prussia had fallen into the hands of the Russians, and Cleves remained in those of the French, these were losses that had been foreseen from the first, and they were more than counterbalanced by his continued occupation of the rich Saxon electorate. On the central provinces of the Prussian monarchy, though they had most of them been the seat of military operations, the enemy had made no permanent impression; the Austrians retained no footing in Silesia; the Russians had retired behind the Vistula; the Swedes, after an ill-concerted incursion into the heart of Brandenburg, had been chased back to Stralsund. But the appearance of strength was in a measure fallacious. The protraction of the war was telling far more on the resources of Prussia than on those of the great powers allied against her. Moreover, a new factor had arisen which must henceforth always be taken into account. Zorndorf was a kind of revelation to Frederick. Previously he had thought little of the fighting power of the Russians, but their steadfastness on that stricken field had shown what they were capable of if properly led.

§2. KUNERSDORF AND MAXEN.

Three years of the war were gone and the ardour of Frederick's enemies showed no signs of abating. The war was unpopular in the Russian army, but the *Czarina* thought no sacrifice too great for the gratification of her hatred. France was sick of it too, and tottering on the verge of national bankruptcy, but Louis was kept true to his engagements by domestic influences and by the unbending determination of Maria Theresa never to lay down arms until Prussia was thoroughly humbled. Undoubtedly Maria Theresa was right. Had a peace been concluded at this particular juncture, it must have been on the basis of the *status quo*. She had everything to gain by perseverance s as it was probable that the resources of Prussia might break down altogether under the strain of one or two more campaigns.

Already Frederick was at his wit's end for men and money. Of the splendid infantry which had stormed the heights at Prague, and stemmed the rout of Kollin, very little now remained. Nine pitched battles, endless skirmishes, severe marches and constant desertion had made great havoc in the Prussian battalions, and the levies from the Prussian dominions were of course inadequate to fill the gaps. Moreover, Austria, relying on her vastly large population, had ceased to exchange prisoners, and after the end of 1759, Russia followed her example. The new levies consisted largely of deserters, prisoners of war pressed into the service, and foreigners enticed or kidnapped into it by outrageous devices. Such men could not be trusted as Frederick trusted his followers at Leuthen.

On the other hand, the soldiery of Austria steadily improved, as is always the case with a power that has plenty of native material to draw on. In artillery she had been superior from the first; her cavalry was perhaps intrinsically as good, and only less effective because it lacked leaders like Seidlitz and Ziethen, the former of whom was probably the finest cavalry officer the world has ever seen. It was in infantry that Prussia had the greatest advantage when the war commenced, as she had still more markedly in the Silesian wars, but this advantage had been diminished by the deterioration of the one and the improvement of the other, until by this time it had disappeared altogether.

Frederick's pecuniary difficulties were even greater still. But for the English subsidy he could hardly have subsisted at all. The treasure hoarded up in the peace had already been expended, and the Prussian dominions, desolate and partially occupied by the enemy, could furnish no more than 4,000,000 *thalers*. England paid the same amount. 7,000,000 *thalers* and requisitions in kind were extorted from Saxony, and from Mecklenburg-Schwerin, and other States of the Empire which had taken a prominent part against Prussia, and the rest of the 25,000,000 *thalers* (3,750,000*l*.) which were needed for the war was made up by debasing the coinage, Every penny that could be raised went to the army, which even in the worst times was tolerably well fed and regularly paid, so that, in spite of the fearful severity of Prussian discipline, many deserters came over from the enemy to join its ranks. No new taxes were imposed, but all civil officers were left unpaid, receiving instead of their salaries promises to pay on the conclusion of peace.

The summer, (1759), was half gone before there was any serious righting. Frederick had got together 125,000 men of some sort, besides garrison troops, but he no longer felt strong enough to take the initiative, and the Austrians were equally indisposed to attack without the co-operation of their allies. Towards the middle of July the Russians, under Count Soltikoff, issued from Posen, advanced to the Oder, and after defeating a weak Prussian corps near Kay, (July 23), took possession of Frankfort. It now became necessary for the king to march in person against them, the more especially as Laudon with 18,000 Austrians was on his way to join Soltikoff, Before he could reach Frankfort, Laudon, eluding with much dexterity the vigilance of his enemies, effected his junction, and Frederick with 48,000 men found himself confronted by an army 78,000 strong. The Russians were encamped on the heights of Kunersdorf, east of Frankfort, carefully entrenched and provided with a very numerous artillery. To the westward, closer to the Oder, lay Laudon, in the most favourable situation for succouring Soltikoff if he should be beaten.

The necessity under which Frederick always laboured of having to deal swiftly with whatever work he had in hand, in order that he might hurry off to the protection of some other part of his dominions and repair the mischief which was almost certain to have occurred in his absence, compelled him to hazard an immediate battle, notwithstanding the strength of the enemy's position and their great superiority in numbers. Accordingly at noon on August 12, after a long and toilsome march circling round the Russian encampment to reach their most vulnerable point, the king led his troops to the attack.

The attack was at first brilliantly successful. By three o'clock the Russian left was routed; several thousand prisoners and 70 guns were taken. The Prussian generals then besought the king to rest content with the advantage he had gained. The day was intensely hot; his soldiers had been on foot for twelve hours, and were suffering severely from thirst and exhaustion; moreover, if the Russians were let alone, they would probably go off quietly in the night, as they had done after Zorndorf. Unhappily Frederick refused to take counsel. He wanted to destroy the Russian army, not merely to defeat it; he had seized the Frankfort bridge, and cut off its retreat. So confident was he of victory that he despatched a courier to Berlin announcing it. His obstinacy cost him dear. The Russians, supported by six Austrian infantry regiments, made a desperate stand on the Spitzberg hill, and kept bringing up fresh troops against the jaded Prussian battalions. The cavalry was ordered up, but Seidlitz, who had saved the day at Zorndorf, was disabled by a wound. The king exerted himself to the utmost, and exposed his person with unusual recklessness. Two horses were shot under him, and a third was hit just as he was about to mount. His clothes were riddled, and a gold case he carried in his pocket was crushed by a bullet.

By five o'clock the attack was completely beaten off. The Prussians were in full retreat when Laudon swept down upon them with eighteen fresh squadrons. The retreat became a rout more disorderly than in any battle of the war except Rossbach. The king, stupefied with his disaster, could hardly be induced to quit the field, and was heard to mutter, "Is there then no cursed bullet that can reach me?"

The defeat was overwhelming. Had it been properly followed up, it must have put an end to the war, and Kunersdorf would have ranked among the decisive battles of the world. Berlin lay open to the enemy; the royal family fled to Magdeburg. For the first (and last) time in his life Frederick gave way utterly to despair. "I have no resources left," he wrote to the Frederick's minister Finckenstein the evening after the battle, "and to tell the truth, I hold all for lost. I shall not survive the ruin of my country. Farewell forever." The same night he resigned the command of the army to General Finck.

18,500 of his soldiers were killed, wounded, or prisoners, and the rest were so scattered that no more than 3,000 remained under his command. All the artillery was lost, and most of his best generals were killed or wounded. The next day he drew up instructions for Finck, pointing out some slight prospect of defeating Laudon, should he advance alone on Berlin; then after declaring his brother Henry *generalissimo*, and directing that the army should swear allegiance to his nephew, he concludes thus:—

This is the only advice I am in a condition to give in these unfortunate circumstances. Had I any resources left, I should have remained at my post.

It is clear that the king contemplated making use of his phial of poison. The enemy had only to give him the finishing stroke, he afterwards said.

By degrees, however, the prospect brightened. The fugitives kept coming in, and the enemy neglected to give the finishing stroke. Frederick shook off his despair and resumed the command of his army. Artillery was ordered up from Berlin, and the troops serving against the Swedes were recalled from Pomerania. Within a week of Kunersdorf he was at the head of 33,000 men, and in a position to send relief to Dresden, which was besieged by an Austrian and Imperialist army. The relief, as it happened, arrived just too late. On the morrow of Kunersdorf, Frederick had written to Schmettau, the commandant, bidding him make terms, and Schmettau, without waiting to see whether the king's affairs were really as hopeless as they seem at first, entered precipitately into a capitulation, and surrendered the city when help was actually close at hand, (September 4).

The rapidity with which Frederick recovered from his defeat is most surprising, but that he should have been allowed time for recovery is more surprising still. It has been surmised, with much probability, that Soltikoff had no wish to push him too hard. As the life of the *Czarina* drew to a close, the party of Peter and his consort Catharine (afterwards the celebrated Empress Catharine II.) grew daily stronger in St. Petersburg, and their policy was directly opposed to that of Elizabeth. But, however this may be, whether Soltikoff was or was not a traitor to his mistress, the supineness of Daun, who with the main Austrian army lay inactive a few marches off, furnished Soltikoff with an excellent excuse for doing nothing.

The loss of the Russians in the battle was hardly less severe than that of the Prussians, though Laudon's Austrians had suffered comparatively little. No rejoinder was possible when Soltikoff angrily complained that he had done enough in gaining two battles, which had cost Russia 27,000 men, and that before doing anything more, he expected the Austrians to win two victories also. Daun's inactivity after Kunersdorf (and before it too) was inexcusable, and showed plainly that, skilful as he was in the Fabian tactics of defensive warfare, he was wholly incapable of a vigorous initiative. Had Laudon held the chief command, the result would certainly have been different.

After a delay which gave the Prussians time to recruit their strength, operations were resumed. Upon the fall of Dresden, Soltikoff consented to march into Silesia and act in concert with the Austrian commander-in-chief. Still nothing was done; Daun's indecision afforded great scope to the superior strategy of Frederick and Prince Henry. Presently Daun moved into Saxony, and the Russians, after demonstrations against Glogau and Breslau, retired into Poland, leaving Laudon to find his way home as best he might, by a circuit of 300 miles round Prussian Silesia.

Maria Theresa, always slow to withdraw her confidence when once she had given it, as was seen in the case of Prince Charles of Lorraine, strove to conceal her mortification at this miserable fiasco, but the popular indignation in Vienna rose to intensity, and vented itself in squibs and lampoons on Daun's dilatoriness. The Countess Daun received a parcel to be forwarded to her husband, and found on opening it that it contained a nightcap.

With the departure of the Russians the campaign would probably have ended, had not Frederick's desire to close it with a victory led him into a fresh disaster, hardly less serious and far more disgraceful than that of Kunersdorf. Daun, with the main Austrian army, was in Saxony. Dresden was his, but the adroit manoeuvres of Prince Henry, and especially a wonderful march of fifty-eight miles in fifty hours, had prevented his gaining the whole electorate. Winter was coming on, and the Austrians were already beginning to retire towards Bohemia for winter-quarters, when Dresden, the sole material result of their campaign, would have fallen again into the hands of the Prussians.

At this juncture Frederick appeared in his brother's camp, just recovered from a bad attack of gout, elated with his success in getting rid of the Russians, and panting for fresh action, (November 13). With the view of hastening the retreat of the Austrians, and of driving them, if possible, into the difficult Pirna country, he ordered General Finck to take post with his corps at Maxen, to bar their direct line of communications with Bohemia. The post at movement was effected against the advice of Prince Henry, and Finck himself, an excellent officer whom Frederick had likened to Turenne, remonstrated against its riskiness, till Frederick cut him short with "You know I can't stand making of difficulties; contrive to get it done."

The manoeuvre nearly succeeded. Daun, struck with alarm, was on the point of hurrying off homewards, when General Lacy showed him how to catch the Prussians in their own trap. When he perceived his opportunity, his dispositions were made with his wonted skill. Leaving a portion of his army to hold the camp of Dresden against Frederick, he surrounded Finck with overwhelming numbers, and compelled his whole corps to lay down their arms. 12,000 Prussian soldiers, with 9 generals, and over 500 officers, thus became prisoners of war. Finck saw what was impending, and should have retreated while there was yet time, but he preferred to risk his army rather than incur the king's displeasure by disobeying his orders. Finck behaved like a fool, but the king himself was mainly responsible for the catastrophe, not so much because of his obstinate refusal to take advice, but because his habitual severity in cases of failure paralyzed the wits of his officers, and made them court disaster by literal obedience to his orders, rather than take the responsibility of acting against them even when placed in circumstances which the king could not have foreseen.

The capitulation of Maxen, (November 23), was no less destructive of Frederick s plans than galling to his pride. The Austrians now retained Dresden, a place of great strategical importance, though the king, in the hope of dislodging them, exposed the wrecks of his army to the ruinous hardships of a winter campaign in weather of unusual severity, and borrowed 12,000 men of Ferdinand of Brunswick to cover his flank while so engaged. The new year, (1760), had commenced before he allowed his harassed troops to go into winter-quarters.

The downfall of Prussia seemed impending. The king's constitution was almost broken down with disease and accumulated calamities. Great discontent prevailed in his army, and even Prince Henry openly accused him of being the cause of all their misfortunes. Unquestionably he had made great mistakes, but no less certain is it that his dauntless demeanour had saved the state after Kunersdorf, and that it was nothing but his iron resolution that upheld it still.

CHAPTER 11

The War in Western Germany

That Ferdinand of Brunswick should have been able to send 12,000 men to the assistance of Frederick, though not a fact of much importance in itself, is nevertheless significant as marking the change which had taken place since the days of Kloster-Seven, when the French had overrun all North Germany, and were threatening the central provinces of the Prussian monarchy. For two years past Ferdinand had held them steadily in check, and after Rossbach Frederick never met them on the field of battle. But for this relief he must have succumbed; his enemies were almost too strong for him as it was.

Ferdinand had proved himself worthy of the trust reposed in him when he was chosen to command the allied army on the eve of Rossbach. After taking part in that battle he repaired to Stade, where he assumed the command of some 32,000 Hanoverians, Hessians, and Brunswickers, and though the season was already far advanced, forced the French to retire behind the Aller before going into winter quarters. In the following February he again took the field, drove them in confusion across the Rhine, and on June 23, defeated them at Crefeld on its right bank. Want of discipline and the inefficiency of its commanders had reduced the great French army to a disorderly mob; Richelieu had been superseded, but his successor, the Count of Clermont, a prince of the blood, was equally destitute of military capacity. After Crefeld, Clermont also was recalled, and replaced by a more capable commander in the person of the Marquis de Contades. At the same time reinforcements were sent to the army, and Soubise created a diversion in Hesse with 25,000 troops, which had been intended to act as auxiliaries to the Austrians in Bohemia. Ferdinand found himself under the crosses the necessity of recrossing the Rhine and retiring into Westphalia.

At this moment, (August), 8,500 English troops arrived from England to reinforce Ferdinand's army. Had they arrived a little sooner he need not have repassed the Rhine. Had they been more numerous he might have carried the war into the enemy's country, but it can hardly be doubted that Pitt exercised a wise discretion in limiting himself to a less ambitious part in the Continental war. It was enough to defend Hanover and draw off thither the strength of France, while England struck a decisive blow at her colonies and commerce.

Before the close of the year new life was infused into the French Government by the appointment of the Duke of Choiseul, the French ambassador at Vienna, to the ministry of foreign affairs in the place of the well-meaning and sagacious but altogether characterless Abbé de Bernis.

The Government of France had for some time been falling more and more into a condition of anarchy. After the death of Cardinal Fleury in 1743, the king, then close upon thirty-three years of age, announced his intention of governing the kingdom himself, as his great-grandfather, Louis XIV., had done before him. But Louis XV. had not inherited his ancestor's energy and strength of will. He possessed good abilities, but was too indolent to use them, more anxious to conceal his ignorance than to acquire information, quick of perception but without the persistence and determination needful to make his will prevail, timid, irresolute and enervated by the sensuality of his life.

No united action was to be expected from a government where the heads of the great departments were independent of each other, and often at variance, and when the sovereign, to whom they were nominally responsible, was too weak to control them, and reduced to intriguing against them in secret, satisfied if he could prevent any one of them from becoming too powerful. The chief power in the realm was engrossed by Madame de Pompadour, who, though for some years she had ceased to be the king's mistress, retained her influence over the bored and listless monarch by her skill in amusing him and ministering to his pleasures The favourite made and unmade ministers, appointed generals to the army, and discussed with the latter the plans of their campaigns.

In this medley of conflicting authorities, Choiseul made his weight felt from the first. Proud, resolute, and daring, he quickly gained an ascendency over the other ministers, and while stooping to secure his position by complaisance to the favourite, he knew how to use her influence to secure his own ends. For the first time since the death of

Fleury there was a Prime Minister in France.

Choiseul's accession to office was signalized by a great outburst of energy. The treaties with Austria were remodelled on terms more favourable to France, especially in the matter of subsidies. Ships and troops were collected for an invasion of the British Isles, while more than 100,000 men were employed in Germany under Contades and the Duke of Broglie, the best generals that France possessed. The colonies, indeed, were neglected, but Choiseul proposed to win them back in Hanover and in England itself. Choiseul came too late into power. Pitt's eloquence had created in England a spirit that carried all before it, and the year 1759 was one of the most fatal in the annals of France, as it was one of the most glorious in those of England. The great invasion scheme collapsed utterly, and in every quarter of the globe the English triumphed.

In Germany the advantage was at first all on the side of the French. Soubise got possession of the free city of Frankfort, (January 2, 1759), by means of a stratagem, securing thereby a most advantageous base for operations on the Lower Rhine, and Ferdinand, while attempting to recover it, was beaten by Broglie at Bergen, (April 13). Contades then advanced into Hesse, and pressed forward on Hanover in conjunction with Broglie. Ferdinand, disheartened by his defeat, shrank from offering battle, frittered away his resources by trying to cover too much, and had to fall back on the Weser. On July 9 the French surprised Minden. A second occupation of Hanover seemed imminent. The archives were sent to Stade, and Frederick expected to see the French once more before the gates of Halberstadt.

At this point Ferdinand made a stand. Nothing but a battle could save Hanover, and by some remarkably skilful manoeuvres he induced Contades to deliver one on very disadvantageous terms. Towards the end of July the bulk of the French army was encamped close to Minden. Contades, with the main body, lay on the left bank of the Weser, with a chain of wooded hills in his rear, and with his front covered partly by a morass, partly by the Bastau, a little stream falling into the Weser at Minden. A large detachment under Broglie was on the right bank of the Weser, and the Duc de Brissac with 8,000 men occupied the passes in the rear of Contades, and guarded the line of communications with Hesse- Cassel. The whole army was about 64,000 strong. The allies lay a little to the northward, numbering 54,000, of whom 10,000 were English, and nearly 2,000 Prussian. The English were commanded by Lord George Sackville, with the Marquis of Granby as his second.

On July 23, Münster was taken by the French, but Contades was desirous of avoiding a battle until he had got Lippstadt too, and so secured his communications with Westphalia. Ferdinand's object was to draw him from his strong position and make him fight at once, and this he accomplished in a very masterly manner. Though on the point of engaging a superior enemy, he had the boldness to weaken himself by detaching 10,000 men, whom he placed under the command of his nephew the Hereditary Prince of Brunswick, and sent round to Gohfeld, in the rear of the French, on the line of their communications with Cassel.

At the same time he pushed forward his left wing under General Wangenheim, in such a manner that it seemed entirely unsupported by the rest of the army. It was, in fact, separated from it by a gap of three miles, and the manoeuvre would have been a very dangerous one in the presence of an enemy of Frederick's rapidity, but Ferdinand judged rightly in venturing it against Contades. Indeed, through all the movements preceding the battle, and in his dispositions for the battle itself, Ferdinand showed that he possessed one of the highest qualities of generalship—the power of reading the character of an adversary, and judging what he is likely to do in any given circumstances.

Contades acted exactly as Ferdinand expected. Frightened by the appearance of the Hereditary Prince in his rear, and tempted by the prospect of taking advantage of what seemed a great blunder on the part of his adversary, he made up his mind to fight. Broglie was recalled from across the Weser; nineteen bridges were thrown across the Bastau, and on the night of July 31 the French army came forth on to the plain before Minden.

The nature of the ground, which was rough and bushy on the flanks, and smooth between, induced Contades to commit a serious error in the disposition of his forces. He placed his infantry in the wings and his cavalry in the centre, cutting the line of infantry in two. In front of the wings were stationed two batteries of twenty-four and thirty guns, respectively; this was another error, for the cavalry and artillery impeded each other's action. Contades' left wing was protected by the morass and stream which had previously covered its front, and on his extreme right, resting on the Weser, a separate corps was stationed under the command of Broglie. Broglie was to commence the battle by attacking the seemingly unprotected corps under Wangenheim; and when Wangenheim had been driven in, the whole French

BATTLE OF MINDEN,

August 1, 1759.

a a, French Army behind Minden, July 31.
b b, Broglio's detachment.
c c, The Allied Army, July 31.
d d, Wangenheim.
e, The Duc de Brissac.
f, The Hereditary Prince.
g g, French Army in battle order, August 1.
h h, Allied Army about to attack, August 1.
i, Cavalry under Sackville.

army was to throw itself on Ferdinand's exposed left flank.

For the success of this plan it was necessary that Ferdinand should sit still and let himself be attacked. Ferdinand, however, intended to do nothing of the kind. Foreseeing Contades' movements, he had made his arrangements with great precision the day before, and at three in the morning of August 1, as soon as the French were known to be stirring, he set his columns in motion. Thus when Broglie began the attack at five o'clock, he not only found Wangenheim stronger than he expected, but to his surprise saw the whole allied army marching up. Half an hour later it was in position, and the gap between Ferdinand's left and the corps of Wangenheim, into which Contades meant to thrust himself, was filled up.

The brunt of the battle was borne by six English infantry regiments and three Hanoverian battalions in the right centre of the allied army, which found themselves opposed to the French cavalry, an immense mass of sixty-three squadrons (7,560 sabres), and got engaged by a mistake before the rest of the army was in line. While the columns were deploying, an order came down from Ferdinand that when the troops advanced it should be with drums beating. General Spörcken, who commanded the right centre, fancying that he was ordered to advance at once with drums beating, set off straight- way with what regiments were formed, leaving the rest to follow as best they could.

With the utmost steadfastness these troops advanced across the plain over an interval of 1,500 paces, with the French batteries playing on their flanks, delivered their fire at ten paces distance, then received the charge of eleven squadrons, and beat them off. The second line charged with as little success. Then the *Carabineers* and *Gendarmerie* of the reserve, eighteen squadrons of the choicest troops of France, swept down with tremendous fury on the unyielding battalions. The first line was broken through in several places, but the second received them with so hot a fire that they also had to retire.

Then was the opportunity for the cavalry of the allies to dash in and complete the ruin. The French centre was in confusion; their left even yet was not completely formed. The charge of a few squadrons must have routed them utterly, and, hemmed in as they were, between the Weser and the morass, with the Bastau and the hills in their rear, very few indeed could have escaped. But cavalry was not forthcoming. On Ferdinand's right were fourteen English and ten Hanoverian squadrons (3,331 sabres), under Lord George Sackville, but though *aide-de-camp* after *aide-de-camp* was sent to him, Sackville could not

BATTLE OF MINDEN

be induced to advance. At length, Ferdinand, in despair, sent orders to Lord Granby, who commanded the second line; but Sackville hindered him, and the opportunity passed away.

Relieved from immediate danger, the French recovered themselves somewhat, but after a tough struggle they were obliged to give way all along the line. By ten o'clock they were in full retreat, but the retreat was covered by Broglie, the grenadiers of France behaving splendidly, and the army of Contades got back into Minden, beaten but not annihilated, as it might have been if Sackville had obeyed orders.

The victory would not have been decisive, and the French might perhaps have returned to their old camp behind the Bastau but for Ferdinand's precaution in sending his nephew to their rear. While the battle was going on before Minden, the Hereditary Prince defeated the Duc de Brissac and occupied the passes in the hills. At the same time, General Gilsen with a small detachment from Lübbecke defeated the Duc d'Havré, who guarded the interval between the hills and the morass. The old camp thus became untenable, and retreat by the left bank of the Weser was cut off.

The night after the battle Contades withdrew his army across the Weser; the next day Minden was surrendered, and the French commenced a hasty and disorderly retreat upon Hesse-Cassel. They had lost 7,086 killed, wounded and prisoners, besides forty-three guns, seventeen flags and standards, and the greater part of their baggage. The loss of the allies was 2,762, of which a full half fell on the English, and chiefly on the six regiments whose steadfastness had won the day. These regiments were the 12th, 20th, 23rd, 25th, 37th and 51st of the line, and they bear "Minden" on their colours now.

Great indignation was felt throughout the army at the cowardice of Lord George Sackville, by whose disobedience to reiterate orders the victory was first jeopardised and ultimately shorn of its completeness; and on the day after the battle general orders were issued by Ferdinand in which a severe though indirect censure was passed on his conduct. Sackville then wrote home for leave to resign his command, and on his arrival in England demanded a court martial. When the court met in the following February, the fact of his disobedience and of his reluctance to go into action were clearly established by the evidence of several of the *aides-de-camp* who had brought the orders and of other witnesses; but the most damaging testimony of all was that of Lieutenant-Colonel Sloper, who deposed that he had said to Ligonier (one of the *aides-de-camp*), "For God's sake repeat your orders that that man may not pretend he does not understand them, for it is now over half an hour since we received orders to march, and yet we are still here. For you see, sir, the condition he is in."

Sloper's testimony was confirmed by Ligonier, who admitted that he had seen the confusion of Lord George Sackville to which Sloper alluded. Sackville conducted his defence in person with great ability and spirit, making the most of a slight discrepancy between the orders of two of the *aides-de-camp*. The facts of the case were, however, too strong for him, and he was pronounced guilty of disobedience and "unfit to serve His Majesty in any military capacity whatever."

CHAPTER 12

The Conquest of Canada, and the Destruction of the French Naval Power.

§1. PRELIMINARY OPERATIONS.

In the great continental war of which we have traced the course through four campaigns, down to the point at which Frederick seemed on the point of succumbing to his enemies, the English have very little part. Their energies were employed more profitably in a series of enterprises, which laid the foundations of the present maritime greatness of England and of her vast colonial empire. The first quarter to which Pitt directed his attention was North America. During his previous administration, he had formed the idea of conquering Canada, but his tenure of office was too short to admit of its realisation, and things went from bad to worse, until by the close of 1757 the French had pretty well made good their lofty claim to the entire basins of the Ohio and St. Lawrence. Everywhere our colonies were hemmed in by a chain of French forts; everywhere they lay exposed to incursions from the Indian allies of France.

Various causes had combined to give the preponderance to the French, although our colonists outnumbered them in the proportion of fifteen to one, and far surpassed them in wealth. If the French in Canada were few in numbers, they were all collected under one authority; while the English were divided amongst thirteen colonies, each with its own administration, and with scarcely any bond of union, except a common jealousy of interference by the home government, which was not altogether unmerited. At the same time the French, being less engaged in trade, and possessing less realized wealth, were

148

of a more martial disposition, and they were far more successful in attaching the natives to their side. Their adventurous spirit, and their open-hearted genial temperament, attracted and harmonized with the simple nature of the red-skins, who were repelled by the cold haughtiness and mercantile greed of the English.

To these influences must be added the incapacity of the English generals, and the genius of the French commander-in-chief, the Marquis of Montcalm, a man of restless energy and dauntless courage, idolized by his soldiers, and possessed in a remarkable degree of the tact indispensable for managing the Indians.

Early in 1758 large reinforcements were sent to America, and the Earl of Loudoun, the English commander, was recalled. General Abercrombie, who then became senior officer in America, was, unfortunately as it proved, allowed to remain, but Pitt, with a wise discretion, entrusted his principal expedition to younger men, selected especially for the purpose, with as little regard to the claims of birth and patronage as to those of seniority. The chief effort was directed against Louisburg, the best harbour the French had on the American coast, the seat of their lucrative cod-fishery, and in every respect a position of great importance. Situated on the island of Cape Breton, at the mouth of the St. Lawrence, it commanded in a measure the only channel through which the French in Europe could communicate with their American possessions.

The reduction of this stronghold was successfully accomplished by General Amherst, but Montcalm, with a vastly inferior force, inflicted a severe defeat on Abercrombie near Ticonderoga, where the French had built a strong fort on the narrow neck of land between Lakes George and Champlain which commanded the route to Montreal, the second city of Canada. Among the minor incidents of the campaign may be mentioned the taking of Fort Duquesne, the name of which was altered to Pittsburg.

§2. QUEBEC.

In the following year, (1759), the war in America was prosecuted with equal vigour and greater success. Amherst, appointed commander-in-chief in place of Abercrombie, was directed to renew the attack on Ticonderoga, and then, if possible, to advance on Quebec, and co-operate with a second force approaching the city by the river St. Lawrence, while a body of provincials and friendly Indians created a diversion by besieging Fort Niagara. The command of the second and most hazardous of these enterprises was allotted to General Wolfe, on whom the brilliancy of its execution, as well as the melancholy but glorious circumstances attending its close, have conferred a renown that will last as long as the English nation endures.

Wolfe was only thirty-three years old, but most of those years had been spent in the service of his country. Born in 1726, he had entered the army when barely fourteen, and had served through the Austrian Succession War with such credit as to become lieutenant-colonel at twenty-two. During the ensuing peace he devoted himself with much assiduity to the study of his profession, and to perfecting his regiment in drill and discipline. When war broke out, he was again employed on active service, and his gallantry on the occasion of an abortive expedition against Rochfort, in the summer of 1757, attracted the ever watchful attention of Pitt, and recommended him for employment under Amherst in America.

Possessed of every virtue and accomplishment befitting a soldier and a gentleman, Wolfe was at the same time altogether devoid of physical beauty or grace. A lean ungainly figure, red hair, which contrary to the custom of the period was unconcealed by powder, and a shy and awkward demeanour, were however counterbalanced by a sweetness and gentleness of disposition, which, combined with great strength of character, high principles, and a chivalrous sense of honour, won the love and esteem of all who knew him. Ill-health, and the hope of enjoying for a time the pleasures of domestic life, brought him home to England after the taking of Louisburg. He was in fact engaged to be married, but as soon as he heard of the honourable command which was destined for him, he cheerfully placed himself at the disposal of his country, and the solemnization of his marriage was deferred, as the event proved, forever.

In February, 1759, Wolfe embarked on board the fleet of Admiral Saunders, consisting of twenty-two ships of the line, and about an equal number of frigates and smaller vessels of war, besides transports and store ships. After touching at Louisburg and Halifax, where reinforcements were taken in, the fleet, with 7,000 troops on board, sailed up the broad stream of the St. Lawrence as far as the Isle of Orleans, a large and fertile island lying just below Quebec. Here the troops disembarked, and marching to its western extremity, found themselves face to face with the beautiful formidable city.

Quebec stands on the left bank of the St. Lawrence, more than 300 miles from its mouth, on and below a rocky promontory formed by

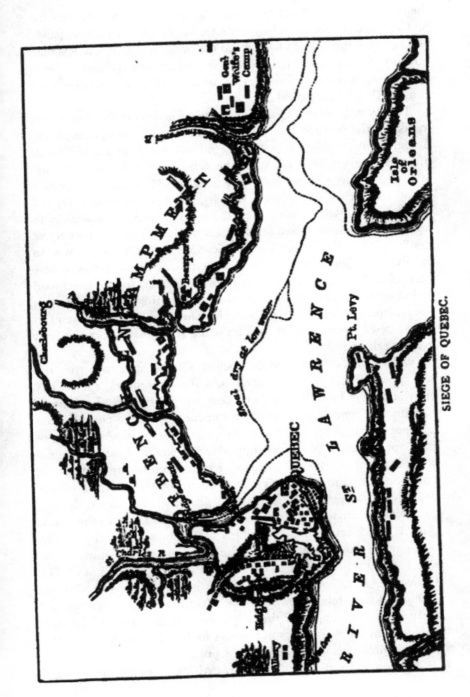

SIEGE OF QUEBEC.

the inflowing of the River St. Charles. Where it flows past the city the St. Lawrence is about a mile in breadth, but below it rapidly expands, and between the Isle of Orleans and the ocean it is nowhere less than fifteen miles across. Behind the city are the famous Heights of Abraham, a continuation of the ridge on which it is built, extending for a considerable distance on the stream.

Twenty miles above Quebec Montcalm had stationed 2,000 men to take in the rear any force approaching it on that side, though this danger seemed excluded by the rugged and precipitous cliffs, which must first be surmounted. With the remainder of his forces, some 10,000, of whom about half were regulars, Montcalm occupied a strong entrenched camp below the city, between the St. Charles and Montmorenci Rivers, with the St. Lawrence and its sandbanks in front, and an impenetrable forest in his rear. A bridge of boats across the St. Charles secured his communications with Quebec. It was on this side that Quebec was thought to be most assailable, but even here great obstacles were presented to a besieging army by the two broad and rapid rivers, and by the roughness of the ground, which, though less precipitous than the Heights of Abraham, was still very broken and intersected by deep ravines, besides being strengthened artificially at every weak point.

Wolfe's first care on arriving before Quebec was to fortify the west point of the Isle of Orleans, as a *depôt* for stores, and to occupy and erect batteries on Point Levy, on the right bank of the St Lawrence, whence a cannonade was opened upon the city. He then transported his troops across the river, and landing below the inlet of the Montmorenci, encamped opposite the enemy. Every stratagem was employed to entice the French general from his strong position, but Montcalm, though superior in numbers, wisely remained on the defensive. At length Wolfe, feeling that the season was attack, slipping away without anything being accomplished, led his men to the attack, (July 31), and was repulsed with heavy loss. The attack had not been well devised, but in any case the obstacles were almost insurmountable; it was a serious error to operate by the Montmorenci at all. The English began to lose heart, and Wolfe's health, always very delicate, gave way completely under the shock. Mortification at the failure, and melancholy brooding over the helplessness of the situation, brought on a violent fever, and for some weeks he lay in a critical condition, during which operations were almost suspended.

As soon as he was partially recovered, Wolfe called his principal officers to council, and it was decided to renew the attack above Quebec. Small hopes of success were entertained; but it operate above was deemed advisable to keep the enemy in play, to prevent his detaching fresh troops against Amherst, who might be in difficulties, as no communication had been received from him, though Wolfe had heard from French prisoners of his having taken Ticonderoga and Crown Point.

Before setting out on his forlorn hope, Wolfe despatched a letter to Pitt detailing the progress of the siege, couched in the gloomiest tones, and concluding with the words:

> Happy if our efforts here can contribute to die success of His Majesty's arms in any other parts of America.

In a subsequent letter to Lord Holdernesse, the last he ever wrote, he says:

> My constitution is entirely ruined, without the consolation of having done any considerable service to the state, or without any prospect of it.

Three days after the first of these letters reached England, an express arrived announcing that Quebec was taken and Wolfe slain.

When all was in readiness, the whole available English force, numbering no more than 3,600 effectives, was transported, under the escort of Admiral Holmes's squadron, to a point some miles above Quebec, on the right bank of the St. Lawrence, where a fleet of boats was collected to bear them to the assault. Montcalm detached M. de Bougainville, with 2,000 men, to watch their movements; but being lured too far up the river by a feint of the admiral's, he was out of reach when the decisive moment arrived.

At one in the morning of September 13, Wolfe embarked on the boats with half his men—all that could be taken in a single journey— and, under cover of the darkness, steered for a small creek a mile and a half above Quebec, known since as Wolfe's cove. As the boats dropped silently down the stream on the ebb tide, Wolfe, in a low voice, repeated to the officers in his boat Gray's *Elegy in a Country Churchyard*, and when he had finished said, "Now, gentlemen, I had rather be the author of that poem than take Quebec."

On gaining the shore the troops found themselves at the base of a steep and thickly wooded cliff or bank, some 250 feet high, up which a winding path, so narrow in places that only two men could go abreast, led to a redoubt with four guns, held by a French captain and 150 men. In the hurry and darkness the path was difficult to find, and the soldiers began scrambling up the face of the cliff as best they could, dragging themselves up by stumps and boughs of trees, and the light infantry under Colonel Howe had nearly gained the summit before the rustling of the branches betrayed their approach to the defenders of the redoubt. Had these been even moderately vigilant, they ought to have been able to keep back a host; but the suddenness and strangeness of the attempt filled them with terror, and, after firing a single volley, they took to flight. The remainder of the troops were then disembarked, and by daybreak Wolfe had assembled his whole force on the heights of Abraham, about three quarters of a mile from Quebec.

Montcalm had, in the meantime, been kept entirely in the dark as to Wolfe's intentions by the skilful manoeuvres of Admiral Saunders, who, as previously arranged, had made a feint against the French camp at Beauport. All through the night a severe cannonade was kept up by the ships, while the splashing of oars was heard in various quarters, especially about the mouth of the Montmorenci, where Wolfe had made his first attack, on July 30, and Montcalm was in constant expectation of an attempt to storm his lines, till a horseman from Quebec galloped into his camp at daybreak and announced the landing of the English.

Then the French commander hurried across the St. Charles and prepared to give battle to the daring invader. How many men he had with him it is impossible to say. He seems to have been superior to the English in numbers, but many of his troops were only Canadian militia. His wisdom in fighting at once is very much open to question—had he waited a day Bougainville with his 2,000 would have been in—but there is no doubt that his dispositions for the battle were worthy of his reputation.

Advancing under cover of a cloud of skirmishers, the French came down upon the English left, drove it in, and forced Wolfe to wheel back three battalions *en potence* to avoid being outflanked. Montcalm then massed his troops on his own left, and fell with great impetuosity on the English right, which was composed chiefly of irregulars. Here also the advanced pickets were driven back in confusion, and a feeling of discouragement spread through the English ranks, till Wolfe restored confidence by riding in front of the line and assuring the men that the light infantry had retired in obedience to his instructions. He then ordered them to reserve their fire till the enemy was within forty yards. His orders were obeyed to the letter.

The French came on, keeping up an irregular fire as they advanced, but our men remained steady, shouldering their muskets as if on parade, till the enemy was close up, and then a volley was delivered along the whole line. Its effect was marvellous. When the smoke cleared away huge gaps were seen in the French ranks. The enemy began to waver, and Wolfe pressed forward to improve his advantage. As he cheered his men to the charge a musket ball struck him in the wrist, but, wrapping a handkerchief round the wound, he continued to advance at the head of the grenadiers, who charged the enemy at the point of the bayonet. Presently he was hit again in the groin, but regardless of the pain he suffered, he still remained on the field, animating his men and giving orders with perfect coolness, till a third ball pierced his heart, and he fell to the ground.

By this time the French were everywhere in retreat, and the victory was as good as won. Wolfe was carried dying to the rear, where he lay supported by the grenadier who had borne him from the field, listening to the sounds of the battle, as it rolled away towards Quebec, and, till his eyesight began to fail, occasionally raising his head to gaze on the spectacle. Suddenly an officer who stood by exclaimed, "See how they run!"

"Who run?" asked Wolfe, eagerly raising himself on his elbow.

"The enemy," replied the officer; "they give way in all directions."

"Run, one of you, to Colonel Burton," said Wolfe, "and tell him to march Webb's regiment down to Charles River with all speed, so as to secure the bridge and cut off the retreat of the fugitives." Then, after a pause, "Now God be praised," he added, "I shall die happy," and, falling back, he turned on his side and expired.

Montcalm was slain too. He was mortally wounded in the action, and died the morning after. On hearing from the surgeon, who attended to his wounds, that he had only a few hours to live, he said, "So much the better; I shall not live to see the English in Quebec."

Five days after the battle Quebec capitulated, (September 18). The garrison obtained honourable terms, with the stipulation, that they should be conveyed to the nearest port of France. The greater part of the beaten army had, however, escaped into the interior, and succeeded in making their way to Montreal.

The rejoicings in England, when the news arrived, were heightened by the dismal forebodings which had been called forth by Wolfe's gloomy letter received only three days before. In the words of Horace Walpole:

> The incidents of dramatic fiction could not be conducted with more address to lead an audience from despondency to sudden exaltation, than accident prepared to excite the passions of a whole people. They despaired—they triumphed—and they wept—for Wolfe had fallen in the hour of victory! Joy, grief, curiosity, astonishment, were pictured in every countenance; the more they enquired, the higher their admiration rose. Not an incident but was heroic and affecting!

§3. QUIBÉRON.

The taking of Quebec was the most striking event of the wonderful year of 1759, but it was only one of a long tale of English victories. Early in the year the French had begun to make preparations for an invasion of the British Isles on a large scale. Flat-bottomed boats were built at Havre and other places along the coasts of Normandy and Brittany, and large fleets were collected at Brest and Toulon, besides a small squadron at Dunkirk. A considerable force was assembled at Vannes in the south of Brittany, under the command of the Duc d'Aiguillon, which was to be convoyed to the Irish coasts by the combined fleets of Brest and Toulon, while the flat-bottomed boats transported a second army across the channel under cover of a dark night. The Dunkirk squadron, under Admiral Thurot, a celebrated privateer, was to create a diversion by attacking some part of the Scotch coast.

The design was bold and well contrived, and would not improbably have succeeded three or even two years before, but the opportunity was gone. England was no longer in "that enervate state in which 20,000 men from France could shake her." Had a landing been effected, the regular troops in the country, with the support of the newly created militia, would probably have been equal to the emergency, but a more effectual bulwark was found in the fleet, which watched the whole French coast, ready to engage the enemy as soon as he ventured out of his ports.

The first attempt to break through the cordon was made by M. de la Clue from Toulon. The English Mediterranean fleet, under Admiral Boscawen, cruising before that port, was compelled early in July to retire to Gibraltar to take in water and provisions and to refit some of the ships. Hereupon M. de la Clue put to sea, and hugging the African coast, passed the straits without molestation. Boscawen, however, though his ships were not yet refitted, at once gave chase, and came up with the enemy off the coast of Portugal, where an engagement took place,(August 18), in which three French ships were taken and two driven on shore and burnt. The remainder took refuge in Cadiz, where they were blockaded till the winter, when, the English fleet being driven off the coast by a storm, they managed to get back to Toulon.

The discomfiture of the Brest fleet under M. de Conflans was even more complete. On November 9 Admiral Sir Edward Hawke, who had blockaded Brest all the summer and autumn, was driven from his post by a violent gale, and on the 14th, Conflans put to sea with twenty-one sail of the line, and four frigates. On the same day, Hawke, with twenty-two sail of the line, stood out from Torbay, where he had taken shelter, and made sail for Quibéron Bay, judging that Conflans would steer thither to liberate a fleet of transports which were blocked up in the River Morbihan, by a small squadron of frigates under Commodore Duff. On the morning of the 20th, he sighted the French fleet chasing Duff in Quibéron Bay. Conflans, when he discerned the English, recalled his chasing ships and prepared for action, but on their nearer approach changed his mind, and ran for shelter among the shoals and rocks of the coast.

The sea was running mountains high and the coast was very dangerous and little known to the English, who had no pilots, but Hawke, whom no peril could daunt, never hesitated a moment, but crowded all sail after them. Without regard to lines of battle, every ship was directed to make the best of her way towards the enemy, the admiral telling his officers he was for the old way of fighting, to make downright work with them. In consequence many of the English ships never got into action at all, but the short winter day was wearing away and all haste was needed if the enemy were not to escape.

At 2 p. m. the French fleet, still retiring shorewards, began firing on the leading English ships, the *Warspite* 74 and the *Dorsetshire* 70, and by half-past two the *Revenge* 64, *Magnanime* 74, *Torbay* 74, *Montague* 60, *Resolution* 74, *Swiftsure* 70, and *Defiance* 60, had also come into action. A tremendous cannonading then commenced, and as long as daylight lasted, (November 20), the battle raged with great fury, so near the coast that "10,000 persons on the shore were the sad spectators of the white flag's disgrace."

Hawke himself, on the *Royal George* of 100 guns and 880 men, did not get into action till near 4 o'clock. When he came up the *Formi-*

dable hauled down her colours to him; she had been subdued by the *Resolution*, but the French vice-admiral was on board of her, and he made it a point of honour to strike to the English admiral. The *Royal George* then held on her course, passing through the French ships without returning their fire, and going straight for the great *Soleil Royal* of 80 guns and 1,200 men, on which M. de Conflans hoisted his flag. The *Soleil Royal* was in the midst of the shoals, and the master of the *Royal George* pointed out to Hawke the danger he ran in following her. Hawke replied, "You have done your duty in this remonstrance; you are now to obey my orders and lay me alongside of the French admiral." After exchanging a few broadsides the *Soleil Royal* sheered off, but other French ships closed round the English admiral, and the *Royal George* was at one time engaged with seven ships at once, but the firing was so wild that only thirty or forty shots hit her, while she sank the French *Superb*.

By nightfall two French ships, the *Thésée* 74, and the *Superb* 70, were sunk, and two, the *Formidable* 80, and the *Heros* 74, had struck. The *Soleil Royal* afterwards went aground, but her crew escaped, as did that of the *Héros*, whose captain dishonourably ran her ashore in the night. Of the remainder, seven ships of the line and four frigates threw their guns overboard, and escaped up the River Vilaine, where most of them bumped their bottoms out in the shallow water; the rest got away and took shelter in the Charente, all but one, which was wrecked, but very few ever got out again. With two hours more of daylight, Hawke thought he could have taken or destroyed all, as he was almost up with the French van when night overtook him. Two English ships, the *Essex* 64, and the *Resolution* 74, went ashore in the night and could not be got off, but the crews were saved, and the victory was won with the loss of only 40 killed and 200 wounded.

The great invasion scheme was completely wrecked. Thurot had succeeded in getting out from Dunkirk, and for some months was a terror to the northern coast-towns, but early in the following year an end was put to his career. For the rest of the war the French never ventured to meet the English in battle on the high seas, and could only look on helplessly while their colonies and commerce fell into the hands of their rivals. From the day of the fight in Quibéron Bay the naval and commercial supremacy of England was assured.

§4. The Capitulation of Montreal.

Wolfe's victory and the destruction of the French fleets made the ultimate conquest of Canada a matter of certainty, but it was not accomplished until after a gallant attempt to plant the standard of France once more on the walls of Quebec. After the surrender of the city the English fleet had sailed away, leaving General Murray with 7,000 men to hold it till the melting of the ice in the spring should enable a fresh armament to enter the St. Lawrence. Under the impression that they would be useless in the winter, no ships were left—a mistake which nearly proved serious, owing to the circumstance that the upper waters of the St. Lawrence are open for navigation long before the Gulf is freed from ice.

The French after all their losses could still send into the field 5,000 regular troops, besides 5,000 militia and a few hundred Indians, a mere handful compared with the force with which Amherst would surround them in the summer, but enough to make a dash at Quebec with some prospect of success before the English commander-in-chief could take the field. Accordingly, as soon as the frost had given sufficiently to open a passage in the middle of the stream for the store-ships and two frigates with them to descend the river, (April 17, 1760), the Chevalier de Levis, though the snow was still knee-deep on the ground, set out from Montreal with his whole force. On April 26 he arrived before Quebec. Scurvy had carried off 1,000 of the garrison, and disabled a much larger number, so that Murray had hardly more than 3,000 effectives.

Common prudence would have counselled his remaining within the walls of Quebec, but prudence was mastered by ambition. Eager to finish the war at one stroke before reinforcements could arrive to share the glory, Murray marched out, delivered battle on the Heights of Abraham, and was defeated with the loss of 1,000 men, and most of his the English, field artillery, (April 28). The loss of the French is variously stated, but the English computed it at 2,000.

The next day De Levis opened trenches against Quebec. All now turned on the arrival of succours. Had a French fleet appeared first in the St. Lawrence, Quebec would probably have fallen, but such a contingency was rendered unlikely by the victories of Hawke and Boscawen. The siege was soon over; on May 9, an English frigate anchored in the basin, bringing news that a squadron was in the river. On the 15th, a ship siege raised of the line and another frigate arrived, and by English the next morning the two frigates attacked and destroyed the French ships. De Levis saw at once that his enterprise was hopeless, and, judging from the boldness of the English frigates, that they were the vanguard of a large reinforcement close at hand, he abandoned the siege with precipitation, and retired, leaving behind all his artillery and a great part of his ammunition and baggage.

De Levis's march on Quebec was the last scene in the defence of Canada, a defence which had been conducted under circumstances of peculiar difficulty, inferiority of numbers, neglect of the home government, and a dearth of supplies amounting almost to famine, but maintained to the last with a gallantry and devotion worthy of the best days of France. Nothing now remained for Amherst but to draw the toils round his prey. In the face of overwhelming odds, the French surrendered without striking a blow, and by the capitulation of Montreal, (September 8), the whole of Canada was yielded up to the English.

Louisiana alone now remained to France of all her vast American possessions. After six years of warfare, a definite answer had been given to the question—one of the greatest of all that were involved in the Seven Years' war—the question whether North America was to be English or French. Perhaps the result was inevitable in any case, and was only hastened by Pitt's energy and Wolfe's heroism. It may be that the greater vitality of the English colonies, and their immense superiority in population and wealth, would have assured, sooner or later, the absorption of their weaker neighbour; but if the absorption had been delayed, even for a generation, the development of America might have run in different channels. As it was, the conquest of Canada soon bore fruit that was little looked for by the conquerors. Within sixteen years of the capitulation of Montreal, the celebrated Declaration of Independence was signed by the thirteen old English colonies.

Montcalm foretold it, if a curiously interesting letter, purporting to have been written by him three weeks before his death, may be accepted as genuine. In this letter he dwells on the independent spirit of the English colonists, and their impatience under restraint, and after observing that nothing but their fear of falling under the power of France had prevented their throwing off the yoke of the mother country long before, predicts that they would throw it off within ten years of the conquest of Canada. His prediction was almost literally fulfilled, but it is a significant fact, and one which Montcalm perhaps did not foresee, that all through the struggle for independence, even when France was fighting on the side of the revolted colonies, the French Canadians remained, as they have remained ever since, unswerving in loyalty to their new mistress.

CHAPTER 13

India

§1. DUPLEIX.

The history of the French in India bears a certain resemblance to the history of their countrymen in North America. Of all the European powers who made a serious attempt to secure a share of the trade with the East Indies, the French were the last in the field, and their earliest efforts, restricted by the jealousy of rivals already in possession, and languidly supported by the home government, were rewarded with scanty success. Nevertheless, as in North America, the tact and skill displayed by the governors of their settlements in ingratiating themselves with the native powers, built up for them a position, in some respects far stronger than was enjoyed by their commercial rivals, and one which enabled them to take advantage of the political situation which arose after the break-up of the Mogul Empire in the first half of the eighteenth century.

Aurungzebe, the great Emperor who extended Mogul rule over almost the whole of what we call India, died in 1707, and his successors inherited nothing of his courage and capacity. They have been compared not inaptly with the successors of Charlemagne. Their empire was already crumbling to pieces, when the invasion of Nadir Shah of Persia dealt it a fatal blow (1739). The viceroys of the great provinces threw off their allegiance to the Court of Delhi, and the Mahrattas, Sikhs, and Pathans, warlike races which had never been really subdued, asserted their independence once more.

In the anarchy which set in from end to end of the Peninsula the French settlements throve apace. M. Dumas, the governor of Pondichéry, (1735–41), mingled so dexterously in the quarrels of the native princes, that, though frequently on the losing side, he greatly enlarged his possessions, without exciting any suspicions of aggressiveness, and raised the French prestige to a height hitherto undreamt of. There can be no doubt, that at this period the French were in native eyes by far the most considerable of the European powers that had effected a lodgement on the Indian coasts. The English of Bombay, Madras, and Calcutta might drive a more lucrative trade, but it was known through all southern India, that the governor of Pondichéry had successfully defied the dreaded Mahrattas, when they swept over the plains of the Carnatic, and that the walls of the French city had afforded a refuge to the widow of the *Nabob*, after her husband had been defeated and slain. The fame of Dumas reached the Court of Delhi, and the Mogul conferred on him the title of *Nabob*, with the command of 4,500 horsemen, honours which at the request of the governor, who was then on the point of leaving India, were transferred to his successor.

That successor was Joseph Francois Dupleix, one of the most illustrious statesmen of his day, distinguished among the many distinguished Europeans who have ruled in India. He it was who first conceived the magnificent idea of building up an European Empire on the ruins of the Mogul, and who with the idea perceived also the means of carrying it into execution, foreshadowing the policy which has since been ours. The son of a director of the French East India Company, Dupleix entered its service in 1720, and had given proof of remarkable capacity in subordinate positions when his appointment to the governorship of Pondichéry, the chief of the French settlements in India, opened out a wider field for the exercise of his genius.

Dupleix had not long been installed in his governorship when it became evident that war was imminent between England and France, owing to the two nations having taken different sides in the war of the Austrian succession, an untoward contingency, for, strong as Pondichéry was against a native enemy, Dupleix knew that it was incapable of coping with an European armament. In direct opposition to the orders of the Directors, who enjoined retrenchment and a suspension of expenditure on fortifications, land and he commenced erecting a rampart along the undefended sea side of the town, but, though workmen laboured at it day and night, the rampart was still unfinished, when news arrived that war had been declared, and that an English squadron was on its way to the Indian seas.

Dupleix sought to arrange a treaty of neutrality with the English settlement, but the Governor of Madras had the same motive for desiring war which the Governor of Pondichéry had for avoiding it.

Dupleix's influence with the natives then stood him in good stead. He induced the *Nabob* of the Carnatic to forbid the English to attack the French possessions on the Coromandel coast. Still, the chance that the English would respect the *Nabob's* prohibition was a frail reed to trust to, and it must have been with feelings of great relief that Dupleix learnt that M. de la Bourdonnais, the Governor of the Isles of France (Mauritius) and Bourbon, was sailing to his rescue.

La Bourdonnais, on hearing of the danger of Pondichéry, had, by strenuous exertions, succeeded in equipping a fleet of nine vessels, consisting mostly of merchantmen pressed into the service, and with these he appeared off the Coromandel coast in July, 1746. The English squadron, though inferior in numbers, ought to have been more than a match for the ill-equipped French ships, but it was commanded by a man of feeble character, and after an indecisive engagement the English commodore stood out to sea, leaving the way to Pondichéry open.

Madras now lay exposed to attack, and was far less capable of defence than Pondichéry. Prompt action on the part of La Bourdonnais would probably have resulted in the capture of all the English settlements on the coast. But, with the removal of danger, unforeseen difficulties arose. La Bourdonnais, ardent, and enter, accustomed to command, and conscious of great abilities and great services, could not bring himself to submit to the superior authority of Dupleix, whom, perhaps, he despised as a mere trader. Dissensions broke out between these two men, which were fatal to the interests of France. Madras was taken, but nothing more. The precious time was wasted; the English were reinforced, and in 1748, Pondichéry itself was besieged by a very large force, under Admiral Boscawen. Its capture appeared inevitable, but the marvellous skill and resolution of Dupleix, who, though no soldier, was the soul of the defence, averted its fall and restored the waning prestige of the French. The Governor of Pondichéry was meditating fresh schemes of aggrandizement when news of the Peace of Aix-la-Chapelle reached India, and Madras had to be restored to the English.

Peace was re-established, and the two Companies hoped that their agents would settle down quietly into commercial pursuits; a vain hope, for the passions roused by five years of hostilities could not easily be laid aside. Moreover, the peace coming at a time when an unusual number of European soldiers were present in India, there was a strong temptation to provide for their maintenance by hiring them out to the native rulers. Both nations plunged deeply into the dynastic quarrels of the neighbouring states, the English at first with no decided purpose, and afterwards only with the fixed idea of opposing the French; the French, on the other hand, with a definite object steadily kept in view by their far-sighted governor.

The time was peculiarly favourable for his designs. In 1748 died Nizam-ool-Moolk, *Subadar* or Viceroy of the Deccan, feudal lord of the Carnatic, and ruler of the vast territory between the Nerbudda and Kistna with 35,000,000 inhabitants, the most powerful of all the viceroys who were struggling to become independent of the Court of Delhi. On the death of the *Subadar*, Nazir Jung, one of his sons, had seized the government, but his title was disputed by Mozuffer Jung, a grandson of Nizam-ool-Moolk, who had been nominated viceroy by the Mogul. At the same time Chunda Sahib, son in-law and relative of a former *Nabob*, laid claim to the throne of the Carnatic, which had been conferred by the *Subadar* on Anwaroodeen, a man in no way related to the old family. Dupleix adopted the cause of these pretenders, and supported it with such address and energy that by the end of 1750 both of them were in possession of the government they aspired to.

The installation of the *Subadar* was celebrated with great pomp at Pondichéry, where, in the presence of the nobles of the Deccan, Dupleix was loaded with honours by Mozuffer Jung, who treated him with the respect due to a superior, and promised to be guided in all things by his advice. He would even have conferred on him the *Nabobship* of the Carnatic, but this the wary Frenchman, who aimed at ruling India by means of her rulers, declined with politic generosity in favour of Chunda Sahib.

The Governor of Pondichéry, the setter-up of princes, had become the greatest man in Southern India. On the spot where his most decisive victory had been gained he set up a pillar recording his triumphs in four languages, and round the pillar he caused a city to be built bearing the high-sounding name Dupleix-Futteh-abad, the city of the victory of Dupleix. This was not done from vanity, but from a deep insight into the Indian character; neither was it from unworthy jealousy that Clive afterwards razed to the ground the city and pillar which, in native eyes, stood for a symbol of the great Frenchman's power.

But one circumstance marred the completeness of the French triumph, and prevented the consolidation of their power. Anwaroodeen had been killed in battle, but his son, Mahomed Ali, had escaped, and still held out in the fortress of Trichinopoly, recognized by the English as *Nabob* of the Carnatic. As long as this claimant remained unsubdued Chunda Sahib sat insecurely on his throne at Arcot. Still the chances of Mahomed Ali appeared very slight. A combined French and native army invested Trichinopoly, and an English force sent to relieve it was defeated, and driven to seek refuge within the walls of the fortress. Its fall seemed only a question of time, when suddenly the tide was turned and the growth of the French power arrested by a young captain in the service of the English East India Company.

§2. CLIVE

Robert Clive, the founder of the British Empire in India, was born in 1725, the son of a Shropshire country gentleman. He was a wild unmanageable boy, fond of adventure, and addicted to fighting, averse from book learning, though by no means so ignorant as he is sometimes represented. At eighteen he was sent out to India as a writer in the service of the Company. His first years there were very wretched. He had no friends and little money. He hated the sedentary occupation in which he was engaged, and pined for home. The climate affected his health, and intensified the fits of melancholy which haunted him all his life. One day he attempted to destroy himself, but :he pistol missed fire twice; then, after satisfying himself that it was really loaded, he exclaimed that he must surely be reserved for something great. Soon after this occurrence he found more congenial employment as an ensign in the Company's army. At the siege of Pondichéry and elsewhere he gained experience of active service, and had made himself a name for daring courage, when the emergency arose which enabled him to step forth at once into the foremost rank of the world's great captains.

Like everyone else, Clive saw that unless something was done, Trichinopoly would fall, and with it the last obstacle to French supremacy; he saw, too, with true military instinct, that the only way of saving it was to carry the war into the enemy's country. He therefore suggested to Mr. Saunders, the Governor of Madras, that a dash should be made at Arcot, the capital of the Carnatic, a large open town with 100,000 inhabitants, defended only by a ruinous fort, garrisoned by 1,000 natives. Mr. Saunders entered heartily into Clive's plan, and placed him with unlimited powers at the head of 200 English troops and 300 *Sepoys* With this force there were besides Clive only eight officers, of whom six had never been in action, and four were members of the mercantile service, who had volunteered for the occasion.

On September 11, 1751, Clive appeared before the gates of Arcot, in the midst of a thunderstorm of extraordinary violence. The garrison, appalled at the boldness of men who seemed to set the elements at defiance, had already evacuated the fort. Clive entered it without opposition, and set to work to repair its defences in preparation for the siege, which he knew he would have to stand. He expected that Chunda Sahib would straightway raise the siege of Trichinopoly and march against him with his whole force. From this folly Chunda Sahib was restrained by the counsels of Dupleix; but he insisted on detaching some of his best troops for the recovery of his capital.

On October 4, the citadel of Arcot was invested by 10,000 natives and 100 Frenchmen, under the command of Rajah Sahib, son of the *Nabob*. The siege was pressed vigorously, and the fort seemed wholly incapable of a prolonged resistance; but all calculations were set at nought by the spirit of enthusiasm and confidence with which the little garrison had been inspired by its leader. Clive's biographer has recorded a touching story of the devotion of his native followers. When provisions had become so scarce that there was a fear lest hunger might compel them to surrender, the *Sepoys* proposed to Clive that he should limit them to the water (or gruel) in which the rice was boiled. "It is sufficient for our support," they said; "the Europeans require the grain."

On the 37th day of the siege, a practicable breach having been effected, Rajah Sahib sent to Clive a proposal to surrender, offering honourable terms to the garrison, and a large sum of money to himself, accompanied by a threat to storm the fort and put the garrison to the sword if his terms were refused. The garrison was reduced to 120 Europeans and 200 *Sepoys*, but Clive rejected the terms with scorn. A fortnight elapsed before Rajah Sahib could resolve to execute his threat. Probably he would even then have preferred to let famine do his work, but his movements were quickened by the approach of another enemy. 6,000 Mahrattas, under Morari Rao, were hovering in the neighbourhood, watching the course of events, nominally in alliance with Mahomed Ali, but not caring to commit themselves while his cause looked hopeless. The heroic defence of Arcot ended their hesitation.

Rajah Sahib now made preparations to storm the fort, and at daybreak, on the morning of November 25, his soldiers advanced to the attack. The day was well chosen; it was one of those set apart for the commemoration of the death of Hosein, days peculiarly sacred to

Mussulmans, who believe that all who die on them in battle against unbelievers go straight to the highest Paradise. Wild with religious enthusiasm, and stimulated by the intoxicating bang of which they eat plentifully during the festival, the Mussulman soldiery rushed upon the fort, driving before them elephants with plates of iron on their foreheads, to batter down the gates. Clive received them with a well-sustained fire of musketry. The elephants, galled by the musket-balls, turned and trampled on the multitudes behind, and, after three desperate assaults, the troops of Rajah Sahib retired, having lost 400 men in an hour. In the ensuing night they raised the siege.

Clive pressed his advantage with vigour. Reinforced by Europeans and *Sepoys* from Madras, and joined by some of Morari Rao's horsemen, he gave chase to the enemy and inflicted on them two defeats; then repaired to Fort St. David to concert measures for the relief of Trichinopoly. While thus engaged he was deprived of the chief command by the arrival from England of Major Lawrence, an officer of great Indian experience. It was feared that the hero of Arcot might not consent to serve in a subordinate position, but Clive, greatly to his credit, cheerfully placed himself under the orders of Major Lawrence, while Lawrence, on his part, without any feelings of jealousy, warmly acknowledged and fully availed himself of the genius of the young captain.

Lawrence and Clive carried everything before them. Dupleix's right-hand man, M. de Bussy, the only man who might have given them trouble, was far away in the Deccan, maintaining French influence at the Court of the *Subadar*. The French were defeated under the walls of Trichinopoly, and took refuge in the island of Seringham, where they eventually capitulated. Chunda Sahib surrendered to the Tanjorean allies of Mahomed Ali, by whom he was put to death.

Dupleix still struggled bravely on. He spent his own fortune freely, and raised fresh levies; he set up another *Nabob* in the French interest, and by intrigues with the native allies of Mahomed Ali detached the Mahrattas and Mysoreans from his side. The English, however, steadily gained ground. Clive's health broke down, and necessitated his leaving India; but the discipline he had impressed on his soldiery, and the spirit he had kindled, survived his departure. Dupleix saw the necessity of peace. In the Carnatic the game was played out, but his supremacy was unshaken in the far more important Deccan. Peace would afford opportunities for the exercise of his masterly diplomatic talents, and men like Clive and Lawrence would not always be at hand to frustrate his schemes.

What he might have done no one can say, for he never had the opportunity of showing. In the midst of the negotiations there came out from France an order for his recall, and with it his successor, M. Godeheu, a miserable creature whose sole guiding ideas were hatred of Dupleix and his policy, and peace at any price with the English. The French Directors were incapable of entering into Dupleix's magnificent plans; they looked for dividends, not for empire. The protraction of the war alarmed them, and they were simple enough to give ear to the complaints of the English Company, who represented Dupleix as the sole obstacle to tranquillity. So the order was sent forth which recalled him home with his great work uncompleted, and that order sounded, though no one knew it, the knell of French rule in India.

§3. CLIVE IN BENGAL.

Dupleix had not long left India when Clive returned to it as Governor of Fort St. David, and with a commission as lieutenant-colonel in the English army. His arrival was most opportune. Two or three months after he landed at Fort St. David, appalling news were received from Bengal. The Nabob Surajah Dowlah, a feeble-minded but ferocious boy, had besieged and taken Calcutta, and its capture had been followed by a frightful atrocity. All the European inhabitants who had not made their escape before the place surrendered, 146 in number, were confined on an unusually sultry night, (June 19, 1756), in a dungeon called the Black Hole, a room eighteen 19,1756. feet square, which communicated with the air only by two small windows barred with iron and obstructed by a verandah. The sufferings of the prisoners are too horrible for description. Only twenty-three survived the night, and these came forth in the morning "the ghastliest forms that were ever seen alive."

When news of the catastrophe reached Madras, an expedition was about to be sent into the Deccan for the purpose of expelling the French, whose authority with the *subadar* had been shaken by the timid policy of Dupleix's successors. The expedition was of course abandoned, and the troops intended to serve on it were placed under the command of Clive and despatched to Bengal with a small squadron under Admiral Watson, which happened to be lying off the coast.

Early in 1757 Calcutta was recovered, and the native town of Hooghly stormed and sacked. This act of defiance enraged the *Nabob*, who had retired to his capital, Moorshedabad, not imagining that the

English would dare to invade his dominions. Collecting an army of 40,000 men, Surajah Dowlah marched on Calcutta, where he was attacked and defeated by Clive, (February 4, 1757). He now became as frightened as he had been arrogant before, and was ready to promise anything; while Clive, having learnt that England and France were at war, and fearing lest the French should join the *Nabob*, as they would probably have done had Dupleix been at Pondichéry, deemed it advisable to grant him peace in order to gain time to attack the French settlement of Chandernagore on the Hoogly.

Chandernagore fell after a stout resistance, and Clive was able to prosecute his designs without fear of interruption from a rival such as had foiled Dupleix in the Carnatic. His instructions required him to return to Madras in April, but he knew that, if he retired with his troops, Surajah Dowlah would never observe the treaty. Small reliance had been placed on his promises at the first, and it had since been discovered that he had been imploring Bussy to march from the Deccan to his relief. Clive boldly decided to remain in Bengal until he had crushed the *Nabob*.

Fortune played into his hands. The caprice and cruelty of Surajah Dowlah had disgusted even his own subjects, and a conspiracy was formed to dethrone him, with Meer Jaffier, the commander of the forces, at its head. Meer Jaffier besought the aid of the English, and after some hesitation the committee which managed the affairs of the settlement accepted his proposals.

When the plot was nearly ripe, Clive learned that one of the conspirators was likely to play the traitor. His negotiations had been carried on through Mr. Watts, the English agent at Moorshedabad, and Mr. Watts had employed the services of Omichund, a wealthy Bengalee merchant, who had long resided at Calcutta, and had suffered severe losses in consequence of its capture by the *Nabob*. Omichund had been promised compensation, but mere compensation would not satisfy his greed. He demanded 300,000*l.* besides, and threatened to reveal the plot to Surajah Dowlah if his terms were not granted; he further required that an article touching his claims should be inserted in the treaty between Meer Jaffier and the English.

Clive then stooped to an act of duplicity which has left a dark stain on his reputation. He caused two treaties to be drawn up, one on white paper, the other on red. The white treaty was the real one, and Omichund's name was not mentioned in it. The red treaty, which was to be shown to Omichund, contained a stipulation in his favour.

Clive and the committee signed both treaties, but Admiral Watson refused to put his name to the fictitious one. Clive knew that its absence would arouse Omichund's suspicions, and he forged Admiral Watson's signature.

Clive now threw off the mask, wrote a defiant letter to Surajah Dowlah reproaching him with his faithlessness, and set out for Moorshedabad. The *Nabob* came forth to meet him with his whole army, 50,000 foot and 18,000 horse, all splendidly equipped and accompanied by 50 heavy guns, each drawn by 40 or 50 yoke of white oxen, with an elephant behind to push and assist it over difficult ground. There were also four small field-pieces served by 40 Frenchmen in the *Nabob's* pay. Clive had 3,000 men, 900 of them Europeans, eight pieces of field artillery, and two howitzers. The disparity in numbers was enormous, and it was then believed that the Bengal troops were more formidable than those of the Carnatic.

For the first time in his life Clive hesitated. A broad river lay between him and the enemy, and he knew that if he crossed it and was beaten, not a man would return to tell the tale. It had been arranged that Meer Jaffier should desert and bring his division over, but now that the time had come, the conspirator made difficulties about fulfilling his engagement. Clive called a council of war, and, contrary to usual forms, gave his own opinion first. That opinion was in favour of waiting and summoning the Mahrattas to his aid. Twelve of his officers shared his views, seven were for immediate action. After twenty-four hours of mature deliberation, or, according to one story, after an hour of deep meditation in an adjoining grove, Clive came over to the opinion of the minority. Long afterwards he said that he had only called one council of war in his life, and that, if he had taken the opinion of that, he would never have conquered Bengal.

The river was crossed, and after a march of eight hours the little army arrived at one in the morning of June 23 at the mango grove of Plassey, where the continual sound of drums, clarions, and cymbals told them that they were within a mile of the *Nabob's* camp. The battle began at 8 o'clock with a cannonade from both sides. The heavy guns of the Bengalees were badly served and most of their shots went too high. The English artillery did good execution, but several hours passed without any advantage being gained. At noon a heavy shower wetted a good deal of the enemy's powder, and about the same time the most faithful of the *Nabob's* generals was killed. Surajah Dowlah was a miserable coward. He had kept all the while in his tent out of reach of danger, but he was now over-mastered by terror, and when one of the conspirators insidiously recommended a retreat he readily accepted the advice.

Clive had made up his mind to keep up the cannonade during the day, and attack the *Nabob's* camp in the night, and he had gone to take a few minutes' rest in a hunting-house in the grove. Here he heard that the enemy were yoking the trains of oxen to the guns. Hurrying to the front he ordered an immediate advance. Little resistance was made except where the forty Frenchmen gallantly covered the retreat. Meer Jaffier, seeing how the day was going, drew off his division, and the *Nabob*, who had suspected him of treachery all along, mounted a camel and galloped off at full speed for Moorshedabad. His flight completed the demoralization of his troops. They abandoned their artillery and their baggage and fled in all directions. The loss on each side was very slight considering how momentous an issue was decided. Of the beaten army about 500 fell, while 22 killed and 50 wounded was all the loss sustained by the English and their *sepoys* in gaining a victory which may rank among the decisive battles of the world.

For nearly three years after Plassey Clive was the virtual ruler of Bengal. The terror of his name scattered a formidable native confederacy, and his quick resolution warded off a more serious danger. Meer Jaffier had been made *Nabob* of Bengal, Behar, and Orissa, but he was uneasy under the thraldom of the English, and cast about for a new protector to deliver him from his oppressive friends. The French were no longer a power in Bengal, but the Dutch held a factory at Chinsurah on the Hooghly, while they had a strong force at Java, and in days gone by they had been more powerful in the East than any other European nation. Meer Jaffier begged their help, and it was readily granted by the authorities at Batavia.

The arrival in the Hooghly of seven ships from Java with 1,500 troops on board placed Clive in a delicate position. Meer Jaffier's intrigues with the Dutch were no secret to him, but England was not at war with Holland. How then could he stop these ships from going up to Chinsurah? He had recently remitted large sums of money to Europe by the Dutch Company, but he was not a man to be influenced by private considerations when the public interest was at stake. He decided to prevent the ships from coming up the river. The Dutch landed some of their troops and commenced hostilities by land and by water. Clive ordered them to be attacked, and every one of their ships was captured. The authorities at Chinsurah, trembling for their own safety, hastened to acknowledge themselves the aggressors, and agreed to compensate the English for damage done, and to reimburse their expenses.

Clive's first administration in Bengal was now drawing to a close. His health broke down again, and early in 1760 he sailed for England. Five years afterwards he returned to root up abuses that grew up after his departure, and to place the government of the three provinces more directly under the control of the Company, but this portion of his life does not belong to the period of the Seven Years' War. It is a curious fact that he had already foreshadowed the later policy of the English in India in a letter to Pitt (dated January 7, 1759), in which he suggested that the Crown should take over absolutely the government of the provinces, and indicated the mode in which it might be done, and the advantages which would result from it. Pitt saw difficulties in the way, and the plan was allowed to sleep for 100 years, when Clive's policy was embodied in the Queen's proclamation of November 5, 1858, assuming the direct government of India.

§4. LALLY.

After the fall of Chandernagore the French made no attempt to check the victorious career of the English in Bengal. It was in the Carnatic, where the struggle for empire had originated, that the contest was finally decided. On the breaking out of war in 1756, the French Government announced their intention of making a tremendous effort to regain their supremacy in the south of India, and of sending thither a large force under the Comte de Lally, an officer of Irish Jacobite extraction and one of the most distinguished soldiers in the service of France. Had this resolve been promptly translated into action it would have fared ill with the English power on the Coromandel Coast, for both Madras and Fort St. David had been almost denuded of troops to furnish the expedition against Bengal. But "to think and act at the same time," which, as Lally said, was primarily necessary, was not the habit of the government of Louis XV. Endless delays retarded the equipping and despatch of the expedition, and Lally never got to Pondichéry till near the end of April, 1758.

Arrived in India, Lally plunged into his work with characteristic energy, and with an impetuosity which, though it commanded success for the moment, drew fatal results in its train. On the very night of his arrival he sent out a detachment to capture the little fort of Cuddalore, and by the time he had been five weeks in India he was master of Fort

St. David, (June 2, 1758), the second in importance, and probably the strongest of Fort St. David the English settlements on the coast.

Lally was very sanguine of complete success, as is shown by his letter to Bussy, whom he recalled from the Deccan to assist in the siege of Madras. "I will not conceal from you that, Madras once taken, I am determined to proceed to the Ganges either by land or by sea. . . . I confine myself now to indicate to you my policy in these five words: 'No Englishman in the Peninsula' ('*Plus d'Anglais dans la Péninsule*')."

Thus far all had gone well. Lally by sheer energy had borne down all obstacles and accomplished half his programme; but he had accomplished it in the teeth of growing difficulties, created not by the enemy but by the ill-will and indifference of the Pondichéry difficulties authorities and by his own fiery and overbearing temper. He had come out to India prepared to find fault. Both the directors of the Company and the ministers of the Crown had intimated to him in the plainest possible terms that corruption of every kind was rampant at Pondichéry, and that he was to put an end to it.

Coming therefore as he did with the belief that he had to deal with a nest of robbers, he was not likely to put a favourable construction on the acts of the Pondichéry authorities, and these were of a nature to awaken suspicion in the dullest mind. Though the governor had known for more than a year that he was coming, and though half of his soldiers had arrived eight months before him, none of the necessary preparations had been made. No transport had been organized, no information collected, no resources provided. Instead of receiving a zealous support, he met with stolid indifference. Lally had an impatient temper and a sharp tongue, and vented his indignation in bitter sarcasms. No wonder that feelings of mutual distrust and hatred sprang up between the commander-in-chief and the governor and council.

Besides all this, Lally knew nothing of India, and his ignorance led him into the commission of a fatal blunder before he had been many days at Pondichéry. To supply the want of transport he ordered a conscription of the native population without any regard to the distinction of castes, and men of all degrees were forced to bear burdens in violation of their most sacred feelings. In the same reckless spirit, not content with razing the fortifications of Fort St. David and the dwellings of the English inhabitants, he destroyed the native town with a wanton barbarity which increased the alienation of the native population, whose co-operation was necessary for any permanent success.

The dissensions of Pondichéry saved Madras. Had Lally been able to march on it straight after the capture of Fort St. David, it must almost certainly have fallen. What prevented him from doing so was the refusal of D'Aché, the admiral, to convey him there by sea (which indeed would have been hazardous with the English fleet on the coast), and the inability, real or pretended, of De Leyrit, the governor of Pondichéry, to find funds to transport his troops by land. With a Dupleix at Pondichéry, it would not have been long before the funds were forthcoming. The summer was wasted in a predatory expedition against the *Rajah* of Tanjore, and when Lally at last appeared before Madras in December, the English had made good use of the respite by collecting provisions and calling in their scattered garrisons.

On January 2, 1759, batteries were opened against Fort St. George, and Lally, in spite of disaffection and want of money and supplies, conducted the siege with great spirit. The opportunity had, however, been lost. The English and French fleets had both departed because of the danger of wintering off the Coromandel Coast; but, before a breach had been made which the French engineers would pronounce practicable, the vanguard of the English squadron returned (February 17, 1759) with reinforcements and stores from Bombay, and Lally had to raise the siege.

For some time after the retreat of the French from Madras, operations languished. Lally had ill health and mutiny to contend with, besides want of money and opposition from the civil authorities, and the English possessed no commander of more than ordinary capacity till Colonel Eyre Coote arrived from England in the autumn with the 84th Regiment. Coote had seen service in Bengal under Clive, and it was he who headed the minority that voted for immediate action in the council held on the eve of Plassey. Early in 1760 a great battle was fought at Wandiwash, (January 22), in which the French lost no less than 600 Europeans out of 1,500 according to their own computation, or of 2,250 according to that of the English. Lally was no longer able to keep the field. One by one the minor French forts fell, and in September Pondichéry itself was closely invested by land and sea. On January 26, 1761, it surrendered at discretion.

With the surrender of Pondichéry French dominion in India ended. The city was indeed restored at the peace of 1763, but it was restored with its fortifications razed, its commerce ruined, and its prestige England gone. Henceforth no European rival disputed with England the supremacy in the Peninsula, and the native powers, helpless in their isolation, fell one after another under her sway. In their struggles against the inevitable doom, Frenchmen were often found fighting by their side and striving to check the growth of the all-absorbing Power, but it was only as auxiliaries that they acted, and after the fall of Pondichéry, France herself never more appeared as a competitor for the splendid empire that once was almost hers.

CHAPTER 14

The Fall of Pitt

With the capture of Pondichéry the last of the three main objects of the war was attained by England. Since the battles of Lagos and Quibéron, the French navy had ceased to be able to keep England in the sea; the subjection of Canada was completed by the capitulation of Montreal, and the surrender of the famous city in the Carnatic left England without a rival in the East. The nation was intoxicated with success, and idolized the minister to whom it was due. In the House of Commons Pitt's ascendency was undisputed. Whigs and Tories vied with one another in supporting him, and for several years there was not a single division on a party question. The expenditure grew yearly, but the supplies were cheerfully voted, though the lavish extravagance appalled the more cautious members of the administration.

Pitt confessedly knew nothing of finance, and as Walpole says, "he kept aloof from all detail, drew magnificent plans, and left others to find the magnificent means." He seems even to have exulted in the magnitude of the expense. No doubt money was wasted, but the magnificent plans could hardly have been executed without waste, and, as Pitt himself maintained, prompt expenditure is good economy in war. And the country prospered as it had never prospered before. Pitt's conquests opened up markets for English commerce all over the world, and the exports which as usual declined at the commencement of the war recovered with more than the usual rapidity.

The only dark spot in the brilliant prospect was Prussia, whose fortunes sank as those of England rose. Towards the end of 1759 the English Government had joined Frederick in making overtures for peace, but the time had not come yet. Austria refused to hear of it, and though France was anxious to retire from the war, and make a separate agreement with England, Maria Theresa would allow her to do so only on condition that England should withdraw her support from Frederick. This was impossible, as Pitt, with no less politic wisdom than honour, had repeatedly declared that he would never abandon his ally.

Negotiations were therefore dropped till the spring of 1761, when they were resumed by Choiseul, seconded on this occasion by Austria and Russia. The English Government sent an envoy to Paris, and the French Government sent an envoy to London, to discuss a separate arrangement, which, it was hoped, might lead to a general pacification; but these negotiations, though protracted through the summer, were as fruitless as the last. Pitt had no very strong desire for peace, and perhaps showed himself too much disposed to press France to the utmost, but the real reason of the failure was that Choiseul had two strings to his bow. If he could have peace on his own terms, well and good; if not, he had expectations of being able to continue the war with a new ally.

Since the death of Ferdinand VI. of Spain, (August 10, 1759), and the accession of his half-brother, Charles III. (Charles IV. of Naples, the Don Carlos to whom the kingdom of the Two Sicilies had been assigned in 1735), the Courts of Madrid and Versailles had been drawing closer together, and on August 15, 1761, was signed the celebrated Family Compact, by which the Kings of France and Spain declared that each would regard the enemies of the other as his own, and guaranteed each other's possessions in all parts of the world. This guarantee was extended to the Bourbon Princes of Naples and Parma (a son and a brother of the King of Spain).

Subjoined to the compact was a very important secret convention, in which the King of Spain pledged himself to declare war on England on May 1, 1762, unless she had concluded peace with France by that time, and the King of France promised to restore Minorca to Spain as soon as war was declared, and undertook to conclude no peace until the King of Spain had received satisfaction from England with regard to certain points that were in dispute. The King of Portugal was to be invited to accede to the convention, "because it was not right that he should remain a quiet spectator of the war of the two Courts with England, and open his ports to the enemy."

Disputes had arisen between England and Spain on several points. Spain complained of the violation of her neutrality by English cruisers, claimed the right of fishing on the banks of Newfoundland, contested the right of the English to cut logwood in Honduras, and demanded the demolition of settlements they had erected there. All these England matters were under consideration, except the second, which England flatly denied, and in any case they were hardly important enough to induce a power like Spain, with possessions far larger than the means of defending them, to run the risks of a war with England at a moment when the latter had become the mistress of the seas. The proffered restitution of Minorca, the hope of recovering Gibraltar, sympathy with the misfortunes of a near kinsman, and the natural fear lest the aggrandizement of England should prove a permanent danger to his own colonies, must undoubtedly have weighed heavily with the King of Spain, but it is said that personal considerations weighed more heavily still, and that he sought war with England in revenge for an insult offered to him nearly twenty years before.

In 1742, Charles, being King of the Two Sicilies, joined the coalition against Maria Theresa, whereupon an English squadron appeared before Naples, and its commander, Commodore Martin, demanded in peremptory terms the withdrawal of the king's troops and his signature to a treaty of neutrality. Placing his watch on the table, the commodore declared that he would bombard the place unless the treaty was signed within an hour. Charles had no choice but to comply, but the affront inspired him with a deadly hatred of the English, and it is said that that hatred was the cause of the Family Compact.

The terms of the treaty were kept studiously secret, but the two Courts took no pains to conceal the fact that they were acting in concert, and on July 15, a month before the Compact was actually signed, the French envoy in London presented to the English Government a memorial in which Choiseul demanded that the questions at issue between England and Spain should be settled at the same time as the conclusion of the treaty between France and England. Pitt was astounded at this extraordinary demand made by a nation with which England was at war on behalf of a nation with which England was at peace, and instructed the English ambassador at Madrid to require the Spanish Government to disavow the action of France, and to give an explanation of the armaments which were being equipped in their harbours.

The Spanish Government, far from disavowing the action of France, avowed and justified it, temporized about the armaments, but at the same time made professions of friendship which deceived the English ambassador, the fact being that, though resolved on war, they wanted to gain time to enable their yearly treasure fleet from America to reach Cadiz in safety.

Pitt was not deceived by the protestations, and having shortly afterwards received certain information from secret sources of the signing of a treaty between France and Spain advised that twelve or fourteen men-of-war should instantly be sent to Cadiz, and that our ambassador should be ordered to demand a sight of the treaty, and to leave Madrid at once if it should be refused. He insisted (and subsequent events proved his foresight) that war with Spain was inevitable, and that delay would only serve to enable her to choose her opportunity. For England the war would not be an onerous one.

No new armaments would be required, and plans were already formed for an immediate attack on the Spanish possessions of Panama, Havana and the Philippine Islands. By striking swiftly the American fleet might be seized before it could get into Cadiz, and its capture would add to the resources of England, while diminishing those of the enemy. These wise views failed to meet with the approval of the cabinet. Pitt's boldness appeared madness to the majority of his colleagues.

Pitt's influence in his cabinet, which had never been so assured as his power over the House of Commons or his popularity in the country, had waned considerably since the death of George II. (October 25, 1760). George had never liked him, and had struggled against the necessity of taking him as minister, but after once accepting him, and especially after he had proved his capacity for conducting the war, he had given him staunch support. When Pitt took office in 1757, he said to the king, "Give me your confidence and I will deserve it."

The king replied, "Deserve my confidence and you shall have it," and he kept his word.

With the accession of George III. a new era in English politics commenced. George II., though he might grumble that "in this country ministers are king," and wonder that the nobles of England should attitude of choose to be "footmen of a Duke of Newcastle when they might be the friends and counsellors of their sovereign," had yet never made a serious attempt to shake off the control of the great Whig families to whom the House of Hanover owed their crown. George III. came to the throne with the full intention of emancipating himself from their influence. Pitt was not, properly speaking, a member of the Whig aristocracy, but during the last years of George II. he had been closely united with its leaders, and by reason of his great eminence he was equally obnoxious to a king who was determined to be sovereign in reality as well as in name.

The young king started with many points in his favour. To the end of his life George II. was a foreigner; he never even mastered the English language or attempted to conceal his preference for his native electorate. With this drawback, and with his shy, reserved, ungraceful manners his avaricious disposition, and his devotion to ugly German mistresses, he was little fitted to be an object of loyalty to the nation. George III. was young and handsome, agreeable in manners and of dignified deportment, truly pious and strictly decorous in his life. Above all, he was a thorough Englishman.

Born and educated in this country, (he said in the speech at the opening of his first Parliament), I glory in the name of Briton; and the peculiar happiness of my life will ever consist in promoting the welfare of a people whose loyalty and warm attachment to me I consider as the greatest, and most permanent, security of my power.

The old Tory families, of whom many at the close of the preceding reign were Jacobite at heart, were able without too great a shock to transfer their allegiance to the third sovereign of the House of Hanover.

Yet in some respects he was less fitted to make a good king than his grandfather. George II., though he hated constitutional government, thoroughly understood his position and always scrupulously respected the constitution, and he possessed a fuller knowledge of foreign politics than any of his ministers except Carteret; George III., moderately intelligent and very well-intentioned, was at the same time ignorant, narrow-minded, and intensely obstinate. His mother, the Princess-Dowager of Wales, either with the intention of preserving her influence over his mind, or from a desire to shield him from the prevailing immorality, had brought him up in the strictest seclusion. He had been surrounded by men of no political standing or experience, who had carefully instilled into his mind the idea that he had only to assert himself in order to place himself above all factions and govern as he pleased.

Foremost among these advisers was his Groom of the Stole, John Stuart, Earl of Bute, his mother's favourite as well as his own. Bute was a man without experience of public life or capacity to take part in it, recommended by a handsome face and figure and by a remarkable talent for private theatricals, a dabbler in science and literature, enjoying a reputation for wisdom above his deserts by reason of his pompous sent: manner. Frederick, Prince of Wales, in whose household he had a place, described him admirably as "a fine showy man who would make an excellent ambassador in a court where there was no business."

For the first two or three years of the reign of George III. the influence of Bute was paramount. On the second day after the accession he was introduced into the cabinet, and, though at first he took no ministerial office, he at once gave himself airs as being the sole exponent of the king's wishes, the sole channel of royal favour. After a few months he came more prominently forward. Lord Holdernesse was induced to resign by the promise of a lucrative sinecure, and the favourite accepted the seals of Secretary of State. At the same time Legge was dismissed from the Chancellorship of the Exchequer, and other less important changes were made.

A violent war of pamphlets had previously been commenced against Pitt and his foreign policy. Bute and his friends wanted peace merely that they might get rid of the popular minister, and pursue their policy of breaking up the Whig oligarchy and extending the prerogative; but there were influential men in the cabinet as well as outside it who objected to the war on public grounds, on account of its expense, and from a short-sighted indifference to the fate of Prussia. Others were willing to join with anyone who would put an end to the dictatorship of Pitt, or, like Newcastle, who failed to see that when Pitt had been struck down his own turn would come next, thought, while gratifying their resentment, to serve their interests by devotion to the rising sun.

Such was the state of the cabinet when, after two indecisive discussions, the Spanish question came before it for final decision, (October 2, 1761). Bute and his adherents, eagerly desiring to withdraw from the war as soon as possible, no matter on what terms, were not likely to approve of a course which would extend its area, and others besides Bute welcomed the opportunity for breaking definitely with Pitt.

Pitt repeated his arguments for declaring war, and added, in the haughty style he was wont to assume, that "if he could not prevail in this instance, he was resolved that this was the last time he should sit in that council. He thanked the ministers of the late king for their support; said he was himself called to the ministry by the voice of the people, to whom he considered himself accountable for his conduct; and that he would no longer remain in a situation which made him responsible for measures he was no longer allowed to guide."

Lord Granville (Carteret), the president of the council, then replied:

> I find the gentleman is determined to leave us, nor can I say I am sorry for it, since he would otherwise have compelled us to leave him; but if he be resolved to assume the right of advising His Majesty and directing the operations of the war, to what purpose are we called to this council? When he talks of being responsible to the people, he uses the language of the House of Commons, and forgets that at this board he is responsible only to the king. However, though he may possibly have convinced himself of his own infallibility, still it remains that we should be equally convinced before we can resign our understandings to his direction or join with him in the measure he proposes.

On the question being put to the vote, only Pitt and Temple were in favour of the immediate declaration of war. These ministers therefore resigned their offices after delivering their opinions in writing. The king received Pitt very graciously when he waited upon him to give up the seals, but made no attempt to induce him to withdraw his resignation.

Pitt on retiring accepted a peerage for his wife and a pension of 3,000*l.* a year for three lives, which for a time impaired his popularity; not that these rewards were held to be undeserved, but because his acceptance of them seemed a falling off from the high disinterestedness which he had always professed and practised. Juster views soon prevailed, especially when the course of events proved conclusively the soundness of his judgment on the point at issue between his cabinet and himself.

As soon as the treasure-ships were safely anchored in Cadiz harbour, the Spanish Government threw off the mask, and adopted so haughty a tone that the English ministry were compelled to demand explanations concerning the treaty with France. These were contemptuously refused, and Bute, after a delay which had enabled her to pour troops and stores into her colonies, found himself under the necessity of declaring war against Spain, (January 4, 1762).

CHAPTER 15

End of the War

§1. PRUSSIA.

Unable to avoid fresh entanglements, Bute was only the more determined to withdraw his support from Frederick. A clause in the yearly Convention with Prussia forbade either party to conclude peace without the knowledge or consent of the other, and it was the constraint of this clause rather than the burden of the subsidy that he wished to be free from. Therefore, without definitely announcing that the connexion between England and Prussia was at an end, he allowed Parliament to break up without renewing the Convention.

In the extremity to which Frederick had been reduced, the defection of the ally, who had poured subsidies into his exhausted coffers and kept the whole power of France at bay, might well have proved fatal had it not been counterbalanced by another occurrence of even greater significance. For more than two years the king had been maintaining a mere struggle for existence, losing ground inch by inch. The year which followed Kunersdorf was a year of continued disaster. The havoc of that great defeat had hardly been repaired when Finck's capitulation at Maxen gave the Austrians a firm footing in Saxony and spread an unprecedented despondency through the ranks of the Prussian army.

Fresh misfortunes followed, increasing the despondency and diminishing the power of resistance. A Prussian corps under General Fouquet was annihilated at Landeshut, (June 23, 1760)—this loss too, like Finck's, being attributable to harsh hasty orders of the king's too literally obeyed by the touchy general—and soon afterwards the capture of Glatz, (July 22), laid the whole of Upper Silesia open to the Austrians. Laudon appeared before Breslau, and the Russians advanced unopposed to the Oder.

The situation was one to call forth all the powers of Frederick's genius, which always asserted itself most conspicuously when the need was greatest. After a series of intricate manoeuvres, the king hurried from Saxony to Silesia, followed by two Austrian armies under Daun and Lacy, each equal in numbers to his own. Laudon with a third awaited his arrival, and Czernitcheff with 24,000 of the Russians, crossed the Oder and watched the course of events. The three Austrian armies surrounded the Prussiansbut before their generals could execute a joint attack, Frederick suddenly pounced on Laudon and defeated him with great loss.

He then wrote a letter to Prince Henry, and gave it to a peasant with instructions to let it be intercepted by Czernitcheff. The letter contained an exaggerated account of the victory, announced the king's intention of marching against the Russians, and begged the prince to do what had been agreed on. The peasant obeyed his instructions, with exactly the effect expected by the king. Czernitcheff had already heard a report of Laudon's defeat, and as soon as he got the letter he recrossed the Oder and broke his bridges.

The victory of Liegnitz checked the progress of the enemy in Silesia, but it did nothing more. Frederick could do nothing to prevent a corps of Russians and Austrians from making a raid on Berlin, and exacting a contribution, though the news of his approach made their stay there a short one. Meanwhile the whole of Saxony was occupied by the Austrians, and Frederick on his return to the electorate in October, found all the strong positions in the possession of the enemy. Daun with 65,000 men was carefully entrenched at Torgau, where Frederick with 44,000 attacked him on November 3.

The battle was long and hotly contested, Ziethen, who was ordered to attack the enemy in the rear, while the king engaged them in front, missed the road by which he ought to have advanced, and when the sun set, the Austrians were still in possession of the heights which formed the key of their position. Frederick and Daun were both wounded, and the carnage had been frightful. Still, however, the battle continued. Ziethen found his road at last, and at nine o'clock the welcome news that the Heights of Siptitz were his was brought to Frederick in a little church near the battlefield, whither he had retired to have his wound dressed and to write despatches. When day broke, the Austrians were seen in full retreat on Dresden. It is believed that if the double attack had been made simultaneously, their whole army must have been driven into the Elbe or made prisoner. The Austrian camp at Torgau was a strong one, but, as Frederick saw at a glance, too small for. 65,000 men to manoeuvre in.

The next year was one of marches and manoeuvres, without a single pitched battle. The war was becoming, as Carlyle expresses it, "like a race between spent horses." Its chief event was the surprisal of Schweidnitz, (October 1, 1761), brilliantly performed by Laudon, who, however, narrowly escaped a reprimand from Maria Theresa and the Aulic Council, for having done it without their orders, an almost incredible piece of pedantry, which, while showing how the Austrian generals were hampered in the field, helps to explain their remissness in making use of the opportunities which their great superiority in numbers afforded.

At no period of the war had the situation of Prussia looked so hopeless as at the close of this year. Probably the king was the only man in all his army who did not despair of ultimate victory. The Russians after three ineffectual sieges had reduced by famine the Pomeranian seaport of Colberg, and for the first time in the war took up winter-quarters in Pomerania, and in the New Mark of Brandenburg. The capture of Schweidnitz enabled the Austrians and 20,000 Russians, under Czernitcheff, to do the same in Silesia and Glatz. The Prussian dominions were slipping from the grasp of the king. Fully half were already occupied by the enemy, and what remained were almost entirely exhausted. Men, horses, supplies, and transport were hardly to be procured.

The Prussian army in the field was reduced by the end of the campaign to 60,000 men, and the deterioration in quality was greater still. The splendid well-disciplined troops which had commenced the war existed no longer, and deserters and vagabonds of all kinds were swept into the ranks to fill their places. The utmost severity failed to preserve discipline, and the low moral tone prevailing in the inferior ranks infected even the officers. Peculation was rife; mutiny and desertion constant.

Under these circumstances the loss of the moral and material support of England must almost entirely have turned the scale against Prussia, but for a sudden and complete change in the policy of Russia. On January 5, 1762, the *Czarina* died, and was succeeded by her nephew Peter, Duke of Holstein-Gottorp, a grandson on the mother's side of Peter the Great, a poor silly creature of coarse and brutal manners, capable of generous impulses, but altogether wanting in judgment and discretion. The foreign policy of Elizabeth had been largely influenced by personal feeling; that of her nephew rested on no other foundation whatever. Peter had long entertained for Frederick the Great an admiration bordering on idolatry, and as soon as he was seated on the throne, he hastened to assure the king of his friendly disposition. Frederick adroitly replied by sending home all his Russian prisoners, whereupon the *czar* publicly announced his intention of making peace with Prussia, (May 5), and of restoring all the territories that had been conquered from her.

On these terms peace was made; but half measures would not satisfy Peter's enthusiasm for his idol, and, without the slightest regard to the honour or interests of Russia, he entered a month later, (June 8), into an offensive and defensive alliance with Frederick, and ordered Czernitcheff, who had been recalled from Glatz, and had got as far as Thorn on his way home, to lead his 20,000 men back to Silesia to fight against the Austrians, with whom a few months back they had been in close alliance.

The peace between Prussia and Russia gave Sweden an opportunity of retiring from a war which she had waged without honour or profit, and by the Peace of Hamburg, signed May 22, she also came to terms with Frederick.

The changed attitude of Russia, which would have delighted Pitt, caused nothing but anxiety to Bute, who cared very little what became of Prussia, but cared very much about putting an end to the war. Thinking that peace could be soonest attained by the unqualified submission of Frederick, he regretted the withdrawal of Russia from the war, because it would enable Frederick to protract his struggle with Austria, and baulk him of the object he was willing to purchase by the sacrifice of an ally. Under this impression he sought to moderate the enthusiasm of the *Czar*, representing that by retaining East Prussia, for a time at least, he could induce Frederick to make the necessary cessions to Austria. At the same time he attempted to renew the old Anglo-Austrian alliance, and intimated his willingness to consent to the cession of Silesia, if the Court of Vienna would make common cause with England against the whole House of Bourbon. Neither manoeuvre succeeded. Austria with some contempt declined to listen to Bute's overtures, and Peter, in great indignation, acquainted Frederick with the underhand artifices of his ally.

Thus England and Prussia drifted apart, and though the breach had little influence on the results of the war, its ulterior consequences were very important, for it was owing to Bute's treachery on this occasion that Frederick conceived an abiding distrust of English statesmen and English policy, which caused him to stand aloof years afterwards, when England was herself in need of his alliance, and occasioned that intimate connection between Prussia and Russia which with few and slight interruptions has lasted to this day, and which bore as its first fruits the Partition of Poland.

For the present, however, the friendship of Russia outweighed the desertion of England, a fact clearly recognized by the Austrians, who gave up all idea of regaining the whole of Silesia, and limited their programme to the preservation of the conquests already made. For the first time since 1758, Frederick took the initiative. On the arrival of his new allies in Silesia, he commenced active operations against Daun, who with a large army lay entrenched on the low hills in front of the Giant Mountains covering Schweidnitz. After several weeks of manoeuvring he had all but completed his arrangements for an attack on Daun's position, when a courtier arrived from St. Petersburg announcing the deposition of the *Czar*, and the recall of the Russian troops.

In the course of six months, Peter had contrived to outrage the national feeling in every conceivable way. His wife Catharine, a princess of Anhalt-Zerbst, was a woman of very remarkable ability, but, instead of allowing himself to be guided and supported by her superior sense, he had the folly to make her his enemy by a series of insults, culminating in a command to decorate his mistress with the order of St. Catharine at a great festival, and in a threat to shut her up in a convent with her son, whom he stigmatized as illegitimate. For years there had been no love between Peter and his wife. Her infidelity had been as shameless as his, but Catharine, while despising her husband, had put up with his coarseness and folly in the hope of one day ruling Russia in his name. It was only when this hope was seen to be groundless, and when her own safety and that of her son were threatened, that she began to plot the *Czar's* removal.

Peter played completely into her hands. Every class was disgusted by his rash innovations. Large but ill-considered schemes of reform were mixed up with trifling and vexatious changes. The army was offended by the preference shown Holsteiners, and by the *Czar's* infatuation for Frederick, manifested by dressing up his guards in Prussian uniforms and teaching them the Prussian drill, while he himself appeared on all occasions in the garb of a Prussian colonel, as if prouder of a commission bestowed by Frederick than of being the commander of the Russian army. The clergy were at once alarmed by a project for secularizing church lands, and annoyed by an order to shave off their beards.

Thus it happened that, when the *Czarina's* plot was ready for execution, no one lifted up a hand for the *Czar*, and without a drop of blood being shed, Peter was deposed, (July 9), and Catharine assumed the sovereignty of Russia. On the day after his deposition, Peter signed a deed of abdication, and was shut up in the castle of Ropscha, where, a few days later, he was strangled by Catharine's lover, Alexis Orloff.

At the commencement of her reign Catharine showed an inclination to revert to the policy of Elizabeth, but when, contrary to expectation, she found in her husband's papers proof that Frederick had constantly sought to discourage his but recalls wild schemes, and exhorted him to treat his wife with proper respect, she experienced a revulsion of feeling in favour of the Prussian king. Still, though she confirmed the treaty of peace with the restitution of conquests, she was not disposed to recommence the war as his ally, and Czernitcheff was ordered home from Silesia.

The order arrived, as has been observed, at a very critical moment. Czernitcheff could not venture to disregard it, but at the request of Frederick, to whom he was well disposed, he consented to keep it secret and delay his departure for three days. In this way the Austrians were kept in ignorance of the loss the Prussians had sustained until the attack had been made; they saw the Russians in the Prussian camp, and could not guess that they were only there for show. On the morning of July 21, amid a general demonstration all along Daun's line, which kept him in uncertainty as to the real point of attack, a Prussian detachment stormed the heights of Burkersdorf, which formed the key of his position. In the evening the Austrians retired towards the Silesian frontier, and the next day the Russians marched away.

Frederick was now at liberty to besiege Schweidnitz, but the place was so stubbornly defended that he did not get it till October. He then made truce with Daun for the winter, on condition of the latter retiring into Bohemia and Glatz, and hurried off to Saxony, which Prince Henry was defending against the Austrians and the troops of the Empire. The season was, however, too far advanced for the siege of Dresden, and truce was here also made with the Austrians; and thus ended what proved to be the last campaign of the Seven Years' War.

§2. ENGLAND, SPAIN, AND FRANCE.

Though successful in casting Frederick adrift, Bute found it impossible to bring the war summarily to an end or even to avoid extending its area. In accordance with the policy laid down in the Secret Convention of the preceding year, France and Spain demanded of Portugal that she should join them against England, the common enemy of all maritime nations, and on the demand being refused, Spanish troops crossed the frontier. Portugal was not in a condition to resist invasion, but at the first approach of danger, her king had appealed to England for help, and Bute, while abandoning Prussia without a scruple, could not refuse assistance to a nation with which England had been long and intimately connected, and which was now attacked merely because it would not give that connection up. 8,000 English troops were despatched to Lisbon together with money and stores of all kinds, (1762), and the Count of Lippe Bückeburg, who had been master of the ordnance to Ferdinand, was brought over from Germany to reorganize the Portuguese army. With the arrival of these succours a check was given to the progress of the invaders, and the season closed without Spain having gained any material advantage from her wanton aggression, while both in the East and West Indies she had to pay dearly for her rashness and duplicity.

When war with Spain was seen to be inevitable, the English Government began to make preparations for an attack on Havana, and early in March an expedition sailed from Portsmouth under the command of Admiral Sir George Pocock. A large English force was already in the Caribbean Sea operating against the French West Indian islands, Martinique, the chief of them, was taken in February, and its fall being followed by the surrender in quick succession of the lesser French islands, the greater part of the ships and troops engaged in their conquest joined Pocock on his arrival in the West Indies.

Great judgment was shown in selecting Havana as the point of attack, for, being the mart into which all the merchandize of Spanish America was poured, and whence the *galleons* and *flota* sailed on their homeward voyage, its capture would greatly intercept the resources of Spain, and facilitate the conquest of her other American possessions. But in proportion to the value of the prize was the difficulty of gaining it. The climate was very deadly to Europeans, especially at the season of the year to which the attempt had been postponed by the reluctance of the English Government to declare war the autumn before. The town itself was well fortified, and its harbour, a magnificent basin capable of holding 1,000 of the largest ships of those days, was approached by a narrow channel half a mile in length, guarded by two strong forts, the Moro and the Puntal. Including the country militia, the garrison of the place outnumbered the besiegers, and twelve sail of the line lay in the harbour, besides smaller vessels; but for some reason or other the Spaniards made no use of these except to sink three of them in the mouth of the harbour, though it would have been almost impossible for the English fleet to force an entrance.

On June 7 the English effected a landing without opposition on the side of the Moro, where the principal attack was to be made. Great obstacles were encountered by the besiegers. The thinness of the soil made it exceeding difficult for them to cover themselves in their approaches, while these progressed but slowly. Water had to be brought up from a great distance; roads had to be cut through thick woods, and the artillery to be dragged several miles over a rough and rocky shore.

All preliminary difficulties were, however, surmounted, and on July 1 the batteries opened fire on the Moro, while three of the largest men-of-war placed themselves close under its walls and cannonaded its seaward face. After a bombardment of seven hours, which produced no effect on the Moro, the ships were obliged to retire with heavy loss, but the land batteries proved themselves superior to those of the enemy. By the evening of the second day the fire of the fort was almost silenced when the principal English battery took fire, and as it was constructed of timber and fascines dried by the intense heat, the flames could not be extinguished Thus the labour of seventeen days was destroyed and all had to be begun again, a misfortune the more mortifying as the army was reduced by sickness to half its strength, and the hurricane season was approaching, when the fleet could no longer remain on that shore without exposing itself to almost certain destruction.

Operations were, however, recommenced with cheerful determination, and by the 20th it became evident to the governor of Havana that unless something were done the Moro would fall. A sortie was then ordered, but though conducted with spirit it was resolutely repulsed, and the sappers and miners pushed on their works with vigour till a practical breach was made. The arrival of long expected reinforcements from New York raised the spirits of the besiegers, and on the 30th, after a gallant defence, in which the commander of the fort was mortally wounded and his second killed, the Moro was taken by assault.

The capture of the Moro made Havana itself untenable as soon as batteries were erected and guns brought to bear on it, and on the afternoon of August 11, after a cannonade of six hours, flags of truce were hung out from all quarters of the town. A capitulation ensued, (August 13), by which Havana with a district of 180 miles to the westward was ceded to the English. The men-of-war and merchantmen in the harbour were abandoned after an obstinate struggle to save the former, and in ready money, tobacco and other merchandize collected in the town, the loss of the Spaniards amounted to the immense sum of 3,000,000*l*.

In the East Indies an advantage of almost equal importance was obtained by the conquest of Manilla, the capital of the Philippines, a group of large and fertile islands situated in the northern part of the Malay Archipelago. Owing to the decay of Spanish enterprise since the time of Philip II., the trade of the Philippines had greatly declined, but the islands were capable of becoming in the hands of an enterprising power a possession of exceeding value, not more for their extent and richness than because of their commanding position with regard to the trade with China and Japan, which the masters of Manilla could control entirely.

By way of offset to the loss of Martinique, Havana, and the Philippines, the French and Spaniards had only trifling successes to boast of, such as a descent on Newfoundland, and the capture of the Portuguese colony of Sacramento, while in Germany the advantage was on the side of the allies. Thus the year that followed Pitt's retirement from office was, with one exception, as rich in victories as any of those during which he had guided the war; but it was generally felt that to him, and not to his successor, the victories must be ascribed. This was not only because it was known that the expedition against Martinique had been sent out and those against Havana and Manilla resolved on by him.

The feeling rested on the conviction that the success which crowned these expeditions was due to the lofty spirit which he had revived in the nation, and which sent forth its soldiers and sailors confident of victory wherever they were engaged. Horace Walpole was anything but a friend of Pitt's, and Horace Walpole writes, "The single eloquence of Mr. Pitt, like an annihilated star, can shine many months after it has set. I tell you it has conquered Martinico."

§3. The Peace and its Results.

The negotiations with France, which were broken off by the Spanish episode in the autumn of 1761, were resumed the following year, and presented the curie us spectacle of the first minister of a triumphant power, suing for peace as urgently as if his country had been brought to the verge of ruin. Bute was incapable of regarding the war from a national point of view. He wanted peace for domestic reasons, and cared little by what sacrifices it was purchased. Far from being elated by the triumphs which shed a lustre on his administration, he looked on them chiefly as possible obstacles in his path. In the negotiations of the previous year Pitt had insisted that conquests made by either party up to the date of signing the peace should be retained subject to exchanges; but Bute, at a time when the capture of Havana and of Manilla was imminent, consented to an article providing that conquests which were not known in Europe when the peace was signed should be restored without compensation.

In the same spirit, when he heard that Havana had fallen, he wished to have it simply inserted in the list of places to be restored, and but for the remonstrances of colleagues who knew the temper of the nation better than he did, he would have had it so inserted sooner than risk a delay in signing the preliminaries by demanding an equivalent. The French and Spanish Governments were not slow to take advantage of his pacific zeal, and raised their tone accordingly. Still, though much was thrown away by the headlong haste of the English minister, much remained, and the advantages secured to England by the peace were really considerable; as also were the indirect gains derived from the war which no treaty could take away.

Preliminaries of peace were signed on November 3, 1762, and on February 10, 1763, converted into a definitive treaty, known as the Peace of Paris, of which the articles were in substance as follows:

In North America the Mississippi became the boundary between the English and the French. The French ceded all they had ever possessed or claimed east of the river, except New Orleans and the island on which it is situated, the navigation of the Mississippi being declared free. They, however, retained certain rights of fishing off the coasts of Newfoundland and in the Gulf of St. Lawrence, and the small islands of St. Pierre and Miquelon were given them as shelter for their fishermen, but without permission to erect fortifications.

In the West Indies they were more fortunate. Guadaloupe and Martinique were both restored, together with some of the lesser islands, so that England kept only Grenada and the Grenadines, besides Tobago, Dominica, and St. Vincent, to which she had an old claim.

In Africa, Goree was restored to France, and Senegal retained by England. All the French settlements in India were given back, but under the restriction that no fortifications were to be raised, or soldiers kept, by the French in Bengal.

In Europe, France exchanged Minorca for Belleisle (taken in 1761,) and agreed to restore any places in Hanover, Hesse, Brunswick, and Lippe Bückeburg that she might be in possession of; but no compensation was made to Hesse for the damage her troops had done there.

It was also agreed that England and France should retire altogether from the German war, and that the latter should evacuate the Prussian fortresses of Wesel, Cleves, and Guelders. Who should take over the fortresses was, however, left undetermined. There was, therefore, nothing in the treaty to prevent Austrian garrisons from marching in when the French garrisons marched out, and but for timely precautions taken by Frederick this would actually have happened. Frederick protested against the betrayal of his interests and the invidious distinction made between Prussia and the other allies of the King of England; but his protests were without effect. The English Government seemed equally indifferent to the fate of their ally and to the reproach of treachery.

Spain, considering how unfortunate she had been in the war, got out of it on easier terms than France. She abandoned her baseless claim on the Newfoundland fishery, and conceded the right of cutting logwood in Honduras, while England agreed to demolish the fortifications that had been erected there. She also restored to Portugal the town of Almeida and the colony of Sacramento. These, however, were all minor points; in more important matters Spain prevailed. She recovered the Philippines *gratis*, owing to Bute's article about restorations, and she got back Havana in exchange for Florida, a district useful indeed to England as rounding off her possessions in the North American continent, but not to be compared for a moment with a stronghold like Havana, the loss of which might easily have been followed by the loss of all her American possessions. Moreover, by an agreement outside the treaty, France gave her Louisiana in compensation for the loss of Florida.

The withdrawal of England and France from the German war left Austria and Prussia face to face, for Russia and Sweden had previously retired from it, and it was hardly necessary to take any account of

Saxony and the States of the Empire. It was obviously useless for Austria to think of accomplishing unassisted that which she had failed to achieve with half Europe fighting for her. Maria Theresa recognized the inevitable, and avowed herself ready for peace; but, that the efforts of seven years might not seem wholly fruitless, she strove hard to retain the county of Glatz, the only portion of Prussian territory which remained in her possession at the end of 1762. Frederick, however, who at the lowest ebb of his fortunes had refused to purchase peace by the cession of a single village, was not disposed to be more compliant when the tide was running in his favour. He insisted on the restoration of the *status quo ante bellum*, and on these terms, Austria restoring Glatz, and Prussia evacuating Saxony, a treaty of peace was signed at the Saxon castle of Hubertsburg on February 5, 1763.

Looked at from a military point of view, the Seven Years' War was a drawn battle as far as Austria and Prussia were concerned, that is to say, neither of them gained or lost an inch of territory. Morally it was a great triumph for Frederick. Austria had formed a vast coalition for the purpose of destroying Prussia, and she had signally failed. Against overwhelming odds Frederick had maintained the position he had conquered for himself in the Silesian wars, and by the splendour of his achievements had drawn upon himself the admiring attention of Germany, and inspired it with a longing for national existence. The result of the war was the overthrow of Austrian supremacy, and the establishment of Austria and Prussia as equal powers, the "Dualism," as Germans called it, which ended a hundred years afterwards in the exclusion of Austria from Germany.

The war greatly increased the maritime and colonial power of England. Under the protection of a navy which had cleared the seas of hostile fleets, her commerce was largely extended in all quarters, and it was during this period that she began to assert the right of capturing an enemy's goods in neutral ships, which formed the basis of her Maritime Code. Territorially also her gains were immense. Not only was North America secured to her by the peace, but by the events of the war a vast field for English enterprise was opened up in India. The French settlements there were indeed all restored, but it was impossible to replace them in the position they had occupied before the war.

The prestige of Pondichéry was destroyed, and English influence was paramount in all the principal native courts. Still the position of England after the Peace of Paris was one of perilous isolation. Her naval power and her claims with regard to neutral shipping aroused the jealousy of all maritime nations, and she was without a single ally on the Continent. Her old connexion with Austria was at an end, and the new connexion with Prussia was broken off by Bute's perfidious treatment of Frederick.

CHAPTER 16

Close of Frederick's Reign

The peace of Hubertsburg divides the reign of Frederick into two equal parts. The first period of twenty- three years was occupied in gaining for Prussia a position among the great powers of Europe. The second was chiefly devoted to securing that position, and to healing the wounds the country had received in the struggle by which it was gained. The war left Prussia in a state of exhaustion hardly less frightful after than that of Brandenburg after the close of the Thirty Years' War, the traces of which were visible for a century. Her population was diminished by half a million. Large tracts of land had fallen altogether out of cultivation. Towns and villages were wholly or partially destroyed, and in many districts hardly a trace was left of human habitations. Successive debasings of the currency, and the absorption by the army of all revenue that could be raised, aggravated the miseries wrought by the enemy. From the noble to the peasant, every class was impoverished. For years all civil officers remained unpaid. The police ceased to exist. A licentious and self-seeking spirit took possession of the people; law and order gave place to anarchy.

In one respect only, in her freedom from debt, could Prussia compare favourably with all the other belligerents except Russia, who was equally fortunate. Frederick had borrowed nothing, and when peace came, he had in hand the 25,000,000 *thalers* which he had provided for the next campaign, should one prove necessary. This sum was judiciously expended in the relief of the most pressing cases of distress. Seed-corn was distributed where it was most needed, and 60,000 artillery, baggage, and commissariat horses were sent to the plough. By degrees the land was again got under cultivation, houses were rebuilt, commercial and industrial undertakings set on foot. Much was done by the king which, according to nineteenth-century ideas, ought to have been left to private enterprise, but the truth is, that the country was in such a state of exhaustion that private enterprise was dead; and the practical success of Frederick's measures may be taken as a proof of their suitability to the occasion.

Politically the chief events of the last half of Frederick's reign were the Partition of Poland, the Bavarian Succession War, and the League of Princes. Frederick's share in the first of these events, and consequently to some extent the event itself, is traceable to the isolation in which he found himself after the Peace of Hubertsburg. Deserted by England in a way which destroyed forever his belief in her trustworthiness, he had no choice but to throw himself into the arms of Russia, with whom, after the peace, he concluded a close alliance. His policy then became in a measure subservient to the ambitious schemes by which the highly gifted young German princess, who sat on the throne of the *czars*, sought to reconcile her subjects to her foreign origin, and make them forget the imperfection of her title, and the crime by which she had become their sovereign.

The Seven Years' War had the effect of establishing Russian influence in Poland, which, though remaining neutral, was throughout used by the Russian troops as a base of operations against Prussia; and when Augustus III. died a few months after the peace, the *Czarina* had little difficulty in seating on the vacant throne one of her discarded lovers, a Polish nobleman of no great reputation, named Stanislaus Poniatowski. Plausible pretexts were easily found for constant interference in the domestic affairs of the republic, and well-considered plans for the reform of its impracticable constitution were frustrated by Russia and Prussia, to whom the perpetuation of anarchy in Poland appeared a political necessity.

Poland was becoming a mere province of Russia when a party of the nobles took up arms in desperation to free their country from foreign dominion. The Confederates of Bar, (1768), as the patriotic party were called from the place of their union, were attacked and defeated by Russian troops, who pursued them on to Turkish territory. Then the Turks, egged on by France, and fully alive themselves to the danger of Russian preponderance in Poland, declared war on Russia, (October 1768). They were, however, unable to sustain the part they had rashly undertaken, and the *Czarina's* troops quickly overran Moldavia and Wallachia.

Hereupon Austria, alarmed at the extent and rapidity of the Russian conquests, threatened to interfere, and Frederick himself was disturbed by the prospect of hostilities spreading. In accordance with his treaty with Russia he paid the *Czarina* 480,000 *thalers* a year during her Turkish war; but in the event of Austria taking part in it, he would probably be personally involved, and might be attacked by Austria and France together. On the other hand, it was possible that Catharine might purchase the acquiescence of Austria in Russian aggrandizement by offering her also large acquisitions of territory at the expense of her ancient enemy the Porte, in which case Frederick would see his powerful neighbours strengthened without any corresponding advantage being secured by himself.

A method of reconciling conflicting interests and avoiding a general conflagration was found at the expense of an innocent neighbour. Catherine agreed that Frederick should recompense himself for his risk and for the subsidies he paid by annexing Polish Prussia, and Austria, (1772), when she found that Frederick could not be separated from Russia, drew back and consented to be bought off by a share of the spoil. Russia desisted from her intention of separating Moldavia and Wallachia from the Porte, and took an equivalent in Poland.

Neither Catharine nor Frederick betrayed the slightest compunction at the transaction; but it was with intense repugnance that the noble and high-minded Maria Theresa consented to become a participator in the crime. She, however, no longer exercised the undivided power of former years, but with advancing age and declining vigour yielded more and more, though with constant misgivings, to the restless ambition of her son Joseph, whom, after he had succeeded, in 1765, to the Empire, she had appointed coadjutor in the government of the Austrian dominions.

By the treaty of partition Frederick obtained all Polish Prussia, except the towns of Dantzic and Thorn, a tract far less extensive than those which fell to the shares of Austria and Russia, but possessing for Prussia a value out of all proportion to its area, because its annexation united the detached and hardly defensible province of East Prussia with the central body of the Prussian kingdom.

But in the king's eyes the acquisition of a province, however valuable, was not more important than the alliance of the three northern powers which resulted from the partition, and was likely to derive permanence from the foundation of common guilt on which it rested; and it must be regarded as a brilliant diplomatic triumph for Frederick that he succeeded, on the one hand, in persuading the *Czarina* of Russia to allow two other powers to engross portions of a country which she looked upon as almost her own already; and on the other, in entrapping Austria, against her honour and against her interest into becoming his accomplice.

Frederick's confidence in the permanence of the connexion between Austria, Prussia, and Russia has been justified by the event, for though the concord has occasionally been interrupted, the three powers seem ever to be drawn together again by some inexorable necessity, and the triple alliance of 1772 is represented in the *Dreikaiserbund* of the other day.

Yet in their relations to one another as German powers the antagonism of Austria and Prussia was during the king's lifetime at any rate, in nowise softened. Opposition to any increase of Austrian territory or influence within Germany was the cardinal principle of Frederick's policy, and Joseph was always seeking occasions for aggrandizement. A favourable opportunity was afforded by the extinction of the electoral Bavarian family in consequence of the death of the Elector Maximilian Joseph, without issue, on December 30, 1777. His kinsman, the Elector *Palatine*, who represented the elder branch of the House of Wittelsbach, was generally recognized as the rightful successor; but his pretensions were disputed on certain points by Saxony, Mecklenburg, and several minor states.

Austria also came forward with claims to a large portion of the inheritance, and lost no time in occupying the districts she proposed to annex. The Austrian claims rested on no very substantial foundation; but they were fortified by an agreement with the Elector *Palatine*, a man of advanced age, without legitimate issue or expectation of it, who shame- fully sacrificed the interests of his presumptive heir, the Duke of Zweibrücken, and consented, in return for certain private advantages, to cede more than half Bavaria to Austria.

The great increase of power which would thus have accrued to Austria was hardly more distasteful to Frederick than the high-handed conduct of the Emperor in attempting to dismember an electorate without the consent of the Empire, and with a promptitude equal to Joseph's, he came forward as the champion of Zweibrücken and the other claimants, and as the protector of the Constitution of the Empire threatened by the Emperor, (1778). After several months of negotiation, protracted by his reluctance to go to war, Frederick crossed the Giant Mountains and entered Bohemia at the head of 100,000 men, while Prince Henry, with a force of equal strength, including a Saxon contingent, invaded the country by the line of the Elbe.

The campaign thus far presents an exact parallel with that of 1866. Then, as eighty-eight years before, the Prussian army, too large to be supplied from a single base, entered Bohemia from Silesia and Saxony, marching in two columns on the important strategical point where the with the war roads from the passes converge, not far from the now famous village of Sadowa. But here the parallel ends, for while Benedek in 1866 allowed the Prussian armies to effect their junction, in 1778 Laudon and Lacy prevented it.

On arriving within a few days' march of the intended point of union, the king and Prince Henry found themselves separated by an Austrian army 170,000 strong, encamped in a vast entrenched position, constructed with all the skill for which the Austrian engineers were famous. Frederick judged the position impregnable, and after two months spent in surveying it, food and forage being exhausted in the narrow district between the mountains and the enemy's lines to which they were confined, the Prussians had no choice but to return the way they had come. Whether Frederick's nerve was shaken and his brain dulled by age, as was asserted at the time by ardent spirits in the Prussian army chafing at inaction, or whether, as he himself maintained, he thought he could attain his end as well without bloodshed as with it, cannot now be determined; but it is certain that his conduct was very different from what it would have been a score of years before.

The affair was settled by negotiation in the following spring. The *Czarina* threatened to interfere on the Prussian side, and Austria found that she could not count on France. By the Peace of Teschen, (May 13, 1779), Austria surrendered the country she had occupied, with the exception of a small district adjoining her frontier; and Saxony and Mecklenburg received compensation for their claims. The disinterestedness of Prussia contrasted favourably with the rapacity of Austria, and though Frederick's action was as much dictated by motives of self-interest as that of Joseph, it was calculated to win the confidence of the minor German states, whose interests for the time being were identical with his own.

Soon after the peace Maria Theresa died, (November 30, 1780), and Joseph succeeded to the hereditary Austrian dominions. It is not possible here to dilate on the character or career of this remarkable man. What occurred in Austria in the first five years of his reign, may perhaps best be understood by comparing it with what occurred in France under the Revolution. Except in the war-office and in the department of foreign affairs, where his influence was paramount, he had been shut out from all power as long as his mother lived, and when in his fortieth year he entered on full sovereignty, he proceeded with headlong haste to introduce the sweeping reforms he had long meditated in secret. The work of generations was crowded into a few years, and the want of tact and reckless disregard of rights and feelings with which they were introduced did almost more to create opposition than the reforms themselves.

Had Joseph been able to execute all that he conceived, Austria would have become the strongest and most prosperous state in Europe. As it was, much of his work perished with him, and when he died broken-hearted at the failure of his noble aspirations, he left his dominions in a state of utter confusion. Much of it perished, but not all. The work was done too thoroughly for the old abuses ever to be simply restored, and its beneficial effects are distinctly traceable in the Austrian institutions of today.

In the affairs of the Empire Joseph displayed the same activity that characterized his domestic administration and encountered the same opposition. His efforts to strengthen the Imperial authority awakened general alarm, and even drove the Catholic ecclesiastical states, which had always held by Austria, to draw closer to the Protestant Princes. Towards the end of 1783, a feeling began to spread among the States of the Empire that some kind of union was necessary if they wished to preserve their privileges and their independence, and this feeling was strengthened when it became known that the Emperor had by no means given up the idea of incorporating Bavaria with his hereditary dominions. It was rumoured that the Elector *Palatine* had been offered the greater part of the Austrian Netherlands with the title of King of Burgundy in exchange for Bavaria, and that he had been won over by the alluring offer.

Frederick then put himself at the head of the movement, and succeeded in forming a League of Princes (*der Fürstenbund*), (July 23, 1785), modelled to some extent on the Smalkaldic League of the sixteenth century, but differing from it in that it comprised Catholics and Protestants indiscriminately. The treaty of union was in the first instance signed only by the three great secular states of the north, Brandenburg, Hanover, and Saxony; other states joined afterwards on the invitation of the contracting parties. Foremost amongst these was the Elector of Mainz, whose adhesion gave the League a majority in the Electoral college, since by the Bavarian vote being merged in the

Palatine the number of electors were reduced to eight, and the Elector of Mainz, as Arch-Chancellor of Germany, possessed a casting vote when the votes were equal.

The immediate object of the *Fürstenbund* was resistance to Austrian encroachments and the preservation of the *status quo* in Germany, but it is probable that larger ideas were vaguely present to the minds of its founders. The mere fact that states were invited to join it whose smallness made them from a military point of view a source of weakness rather than strength shows that something more than a defensive alliance was intended; and indeed there is good reason for believing that a complete reorganization of Germany was contemplated, involving perhaps even the abolition of the Imperial throne or its transfer from Vienna to Berlin. Great ideas certainly—but requiring a Frederick for their realization, if even he could have accomplished it, and when the time came a Frederick was not found.

The old king's end was drawing near. A few weeks after the conclusion of the treaty with Hanover and Saxony, he caught a severe cold at a review in Silesia, where he sat on horseback for six hours in a drenching rain without even putting on a cloak. From this chill he never recovered. His constitution was ruined already, and all through the winter his health declined. Yet with failing strength his devotion to the public service never relaxed. Every morning at half-past four his three cabinet secretaries came to receive his answers to the petitions and letters which had arrived; every evening they brought for his signature the replies composed according to the instructions he had dictated in the morning.

On August 15, 1786, the secretaries came as usual. The king did not wake till eleven, but then went through everything with his usual clearness. In the evening he signed the letters; then fell into a kind of stupor. Towards noon the next day he roused himself, and tried to give the Parole for the Commandant of Potsdam, but the effort was beyond him. The following morning soon after two o'clock he died, (August 17, 1786). He was seventy-four years old, and he had reigned forty-six.

The formation of the *Fürstenbund* fittingly closes Frederick's life, and rounds off his career. His was not the fate which has sometimes befallen great men of being cut off by untimely death in the midst of his labours. He died full of years and with his work accomplished. He had found Prussia the weakest and by far the smallest of the great European powers, and he left her their acknowledged equal in strength and reputation. He had broken the Austrian supremacy in Germany, and taught the German nation to look up to Prussia as its natural leader, while his latest political action provided machinery by which, if his immediate successors had inherited his capacity, the time when the leadership was obtained might have been anticipated by a considerable period. It is strange but characteristic that it was only from Austria that he apprehended danger to his own country or to Germany. He could not conceive a situation entirely different from that with which he was acquainted. Events were rapidly approaching by which the whole social and political condition of Europe was altered. Yet, though signs of it were everywhere to be seen, the old king, with all his shrewdness, had no presentiment of the coming change. Perhaps the very clearness with which he perceived everything within the visible horizon prevented his guessing at what lay beyond it. Anyhow, it is remarkable that though he lived up to its very verge, he died without the faintest suspicion that the French Revolution was at hand.

LEONAUR

ALSO FROM LEONAUR
AVAILABLE IN SOFTCOVER OR HARDCOVER WITH DUST JACKET

IRON TIMES WITH THE GUARDS *by An O. E. (G. P. A. Fildes)*—The Experiences of an Officer of the Coldstream Guards on the Western Front During the First World War.

THE GREAT WAR IN THE MIDDLE EAST: 1 *by W. T. Massey*—The Desert Campaigns & How Jerusalem Was Won---two classic accounts in one volume.

THE GREAT WAR IN THE MIDDLE EAST: 2 *by W. T. Massey*—Allenby's Final Triumph.

SMITH-DORRIEN *by Horace Smith-Dorrien*—Isandlwhana to the Great War.

1914 *by Sir John French*—The Early Campaigns of the Great War by the British Commander.

GRENADIER *by E. R. M. Fryer*—The Recollections of an Officer of the Grenadier Guards throughout the Great War on the Western Front.

BATTLE, CAPTURE & ESCAPE *by George Pearson*—The Experiences of a Canadian Light Infantryman During the Great War.

DIGGERS AT WAR *by R. Hugh Knyvett & G. P. Cuttriss*—"Over There" With the Australians by R. Hugh Knyvett and Over the Top With the Third Australian Division by G. P. Cuttriss. Accounts of Australians During the Great War in the Middle East, at Gallipoli and on the Western Front.

HEAVY FIGHTING BEFORE US *by George Brenton Laurie*—The Letters of an Officer of the Royal Irish Rifles on the Western Front During the Great War.

THE CAMELIERS *by Oliver Hogue*—A Classic Account of the Australians of the Imperial Camel Corps During the First World War in the Middle East.

RED DUST *by Donald Black*—A Classic Account of Australian Light Horsemen in Palestine During the First World War.

THE LEAN, BROWN MEN *by Angus Buchanan*—Experiences in East Africa During the Great War with the 25th Royal Fusiliers—the Legion of Frontiersmen.

THE NIGERIAN REGIMENT IN EAST AFRICA *by W. D. Downes*—On Campaign During the Great War 1916-1918.

THE 'DIE-HARDS' IN SIBERIA *by John Ward*—With the Middlesex Regiment Against the Bolsheviks 1918-19.

LEONAUR

ALSO FROM LEONAUR

AVAILABLE IN SOFTCOVER OR HARDCOVER WITH DUST JACKET

FARAWAY CAMPAIGN *by F. James*—Experiences of an Indian Army Cavalry Officer in Persia & Russia During the Great War.

REVOLT IN THE DESERT *by T. E. Lawrence*—An account of the experiences of one remarkable British officer's war from his own perspective.

MACHINE-GUN SQUADRON *by A. M. G.*—The 20th Machine Gunners from British Yeomanry Regiments in the Middle East Campaign of the First World War.

A GUNNER'S CRUSADE *by Antony Bluett*—The Campaign in the Desert, Palestine & Syria as Experienced by the Honourable Artillery Company During the Great War .

DESPATCH RIDER *by W. H. L. Watson*—The Experiences of a British Army Motorcycle Despatch Rider During the Opening Battles of the Great War in Europe.

TIGERS ALONG THE TIGRIS *by E. J. Thompson*—The Leicestershire Regiment in Mesopotamia During the First World War.

HEARTS & DRAGONS *by Charles R. M. F. Crutwell*—The 4th Royal Berkshire Regiment in France and Italy During the Great War, 1914-1918.

INFANTRY BRIGADE: 1914 *by John Ward*—The Diary of a Commander of the 15th Infantry Brigade, 5th Division, British Army, During the Retreat from Mons.

DOING OUR 'BIT' *by Ian Hay*—Two Classic Accounts of the Men of Kitchener's 'New Army' During the Great War including *The First 100,000* & *All In It*.

AN EYE IN THE STORM *by Arthur Ruhl*—An American War Correspondent's Experiences of the First World War from the Western Front to Gallipoli-and Beyond.

STAND & FALL *by Joe Cassells*—With the Middlesex Regiment Against the Bolsheviks 1918-19.

RIFLEMAN MACGILL'S WAR *by Patrick MacGill*—A Soldier of the London Irish During the Great War in Europe including *The Amateur Army*, *The Red Horizon* & *The Great Push*.

WITH THE GUNS *by C. A. Rose & Hugh Dalton*—Two First Hand Accounts of British Gunners at War in Europe During World War 1- Three Years in France with the Guns and With the British Guns in Italy.

THE BUSH WAR DOCTOR *by Robert V. Dolbey*—The Experiences of a British Army Doctor During the East African Campaign of the First World War.

LEONAUR

ALSO FROM LEONAUR
AVAILABLE IN SOFTCOVER OR HARDCOVER WITH DUST JACKET

THE 9TH—THE KING'S (LIVERPOOL REGIMENT) IN THE GREAT WAR 1914 - 1918 *by Enos H. G. Roberts*—Mersey to mud—war and Liverpool men.

THE GAMBARDIER *by Mark Severn*—The experiences of a battery of Heavy artillery on the Western Front during the First World War.

FROM MESSINES TO THIRD YPRES *by Thomas Floyd*—A personal account of the First World War on the Western front by a 2/5th Lancashire Fusilier.

THE IRISH GUARDS IN THE GREAT WAR - VOLUME 1 *by Rudyard Kipling*—Edited and Compiled from Their Diaries and Papers—The First Battalion.

THE IRISH GUARDS IN THE GREAT WAR - VOLUME 1 *by Rudyard Kipling*—Edited and Compiled from Their Diaries and Papers—The Second Battalion.

ARMOURED CARS IN EDEN *by K. Roosevelt*—An American President's son serving in Rolls Royce armoured cars with the British in Mesopatamia & with the American Artillery in France during the First World War.

CHASSEUR OF 1914 *by Marcel Dupont*—Experiences of the twilight of the French Light Cavalry by a young officer during the early battles of the great war in Europe.

TROOP HORSE & TRENCH *by R.A. Lloyd*—The experiences of a British Lifeguardsman of the household cavalry fighting on the western front during the First World War 1914-18.

THE EAST AFRICAN MOUNTED RIFLES *by C.J. Wilson*—Experiences of the campaign in the East African bush during the First World War.

THE LONG PATROL *by George Berrie*—A Novel of Light Horsemen from Gallipoli to the Palestine campaign of the First World War.

THE FIGHTING CAMELIERS *by Frank Reid*—The exploits of the Imperial Camel Corps in the desert and Palestine campaigns of the First World War.

STEEL CHARIOTS IN THE DESERT *by S. C. Rolls*—The first world war experiences of a Rolls Royce armoured car driver with the Duke of Westminster in Libya and in Arabia with T.E. Lawrence.

WITH THE IMPERIAL CAMEL CORPS IN THE GREAT WAR *by Geoffrey Inchbald*—The story of a serving officer with the British 2nd battalion against the Senussi and during the Palestine campaign.